agelman´s Citibank Murray's Superior Pomade Les Mills NBA Harvest premium cider Bluetooth Huffer Tetris Bonnie McKee Vogel's bread

iZona Green Tea SPEIGHT'S Louis Vuitton Eleni's cookies Clinique Speedo Comet Queer Eye for th

ickies Segway Reef footwear Canada Clairol Jones soda Tillamook Cheese eBay Miller Lite Breyers ice cream Target Dell ASICS Kodak

nnox J. Lindeberg Teva Kawasaki REAL skateboards Pepsi Crabtree & Evelyn Milka Iberia PBS Brunello di Montalcino Diesel Burt's Bees

ndaberg Ginger Beer The New Yorker Birkenstock Rolex Gilbert Puma Toll House cookies Tide Fender Stratocaster iPod JetBlue Airways

kia Madonna Yorkshire pudding Lay's Mambo Mikimoto pearls Canterbury clothing Post-it Notes Griffins biscuits Mont Blanc Wolford

on and Garfunkel Origins Global knives Cartier Pantone Lacoste Galaxy Manchester City Xerox Dunkin' Donuts IKEA Wales Oil of Olay

Castle lager Paulo Coelho Dos Pinos The Edge radio station Statue of the Virgin Mary, Harissa A-Treat cream soda Quiksilver Real Madrid

McVitie's Mandarina Duck 7 UP La Alhambra Southwest Airlines The Beatles Peet's Coffee Vernors ginger ale Prime Superman Oakley

ise Cheerios Santa Cruz boards Casio Armani Ernst & Young Meica Julio Iglesias Vans Smart Wool Coopers ale Star Wars Cirque du Soleil

F NAF London Transport Club Monaco Food Network Converse M.I.L.K. Victoria Bitter Where the Wild Things Are Nivea Campbell's soup

outh Africa Tiffany's Sid Dickens Memory Blocks Qantas Bavaria beer Amazon.com Zomba records Toronto Maple Leafs Mt. Kilimanjaro

m Victoria's Secret Boost juice Helmut Lang The Star Alliance Marilyn Monroe Cannondale bicycles Kruger National Park Cabo de Penas

eckham Leatherman Radio Dimensione Suono Opel Cola Cao Leica Commodore Chapstick Mr. Clean De Efteling Laphroaig CBS Playboy

herica Nirvana Samsung DirecTV Channelock tools Ranger Gustavo Broadway Rock 'n' Roll Hershey's Netflix Cleveland Browns Strobe

ga ovens Tabasco Chanel No. 5 Snaidero Guinness Tonga Harry Potter Hibernian FC Venice bobby pins Nelson Mandela Curious George

Upper Deck hockey cards Oreo cookies Renault Clio Veuve Cliquot The Statue of Liberty Levi's MSN Messenger Chopard The Dalai Lama

Movement Wrigley's Salon.com Elvis Presley Whittakers Reese's Peanut Butter Cups Bernard Callebaut Starship Children's Hospital Corona

lefonica Hermès Winnipeg Blue Bombers Iceland Mozilla Dire Straits LiveJournal Chupa-Chups The Tango Quemalestamos Productions

toria magazine OnWar Fujiya hotel The Red Cross SHIPS Celestial Seasonings El Pais Tip Top ice cream Kelly's potato chips Roots clothing

use Light Up The World Foundation Toyota Vegemite God Smashing Pumpkins Original Tommy's Burger Satch jeans Loewen windows

ew York City Captain Morgan's spiced rum Frijoles Don Pedro BAPE Kiwi shoe polish Emmitt Smith Chicago Cubs Bike Friday BMW TriBeCa

-Z-Boy Salsa Lizano Carhartt Imperial beer Palm Pilot Munster Cadbury Teletica Canal 7 Starbucks Lexus Disneyland The Smiths Motorola

lla Sony Gucci All Blacks rugby team Le Pescadou Steinway Hungary John Lewis stores Boston Red Sox Dean & Deluca adidas Originals

rari University of Kentucky basketball team James Bond Marmite Guggenheim Bilbao Häagen-Dazs Evian Cambridge University Pampers

St. Tropez M·A·C Fnac Sri Ravi Shankar Clinique Titleist Sydney Opera House Oscar synth REMO Chestnut Prospector canoe Fijian Sevens

berts Nike U2 XXXX beer Kenneth Cole New Orleans A-Channel, Canada Sedona, Arizona Mercedes Smart Custo-Barcelona Virgin Atlantic

ive oil Audi Bendon Britten motorcycle Gap The Body Shop Harry's Cafe de Wheels Brigitte Bardot Manchester United Ducati Havaianas

d Spice New Zealand Edge Squaresoft Kartell Tods Leite Moça Volkswagen Beetle MTV Brazilian football team Hello Kitty Vespa Swatch

mbro San Benedetto Frizzante Tenzan onsen Chanel Egoiste J.Crew Marsiglia Soaps The NTI W.&L.T. Fado UPS TINTIN your Lovemark here

the future beyond brands

lovemarks

KEVIN ROBERTS, CEO WORLDWIDE, SAATCHI & SAATCHI
Foreword by A.G. Lafley, Chairman, President, and Chief Executive, Procter & Gamble

 **powerHouse Books New York, NY**

"I have learned, based on my experience, that everything is dominated by the market. So whenever we are struck with any obstacles or difficulties, I always say to myself: 'Listen to the market, listen to the voice of the customer.' That's the fundamental essence of marketing. Always, we have to come back to the market, back to the customer. That is the Toyota way.

"So, whenever we're stuck, we always go back to the basics. Because branding, image, or Lovemarks are determined by the customers, not us. We really cannot determine anything. The customer does that. That is the essence."

石坂 芳男

Yoshio Ishizaka, Executive Vice President, Member of the Board, Toyota Motor Corporation

The Beatles

"Yesterday," "Something," "Imagine," "Eleanor Rigby," "A Hard Day's Night," "Lucy in the Sky with Diamonds," "Strawberry Fields Forever," "Hey Jude," "If I Fell," "Nowhere Man," "The Long and Winding Road," looking through a "Glass Onion," "Blackbird" singing in the dead of night, "We Can Work it Out," "Help!," "I Want to Hold your Hand," "Sgt. Pepper's Lonely Hearts Club Band," "Yellow Submarine," "I'll Follow the Sun," "She Loves You" Yeh, Yeh, Yeh, "Michelle."…Nothing more needs to be said.

[Designer, New Zealand]

President Avenue Fruitworld

There's a greengrocer near where I live that isn't the closest, but is the one I prefer to go to. The produce is generally good, but it's more than that–the whole *feeling* of the place works on me. The smell of fresh produce (coriander, pineapples, mangoes...) is fantastic. The owners' Italian accents. And to top it off, they bought the first box of mangoes at this year's traditional charity auction–$36,000 [AU] for a dozen pieces of fruit!

[Copywriter, Australia]

Salsa Lizano

Our *tamales* and *gallo pinto* taste better with it; actually, they don't taste good at all without it. Salsa Lizano is a Lovemark in Costa Rica due to tradition and taste, the fact that it is ours and that we make it with the ingredients of our land. *Ticos* [Costa Ricans] living anywhere in the world can show you a bottle of Salsa Lizano in their kitchen, kept as a treasure from our birthplace.

[M.B.A. student, Costa Rica]

Amul

A brand of dairy products ranging from butter to ice cream. Amul has been around for many decades, symbolized by its cute mascot, the "Utterly Butterly" Amul girl with her witty comments on current affairs across the globe. It has diversified over time to include a host of food products beyond dairy, and is a household name in India. Amul has transcended its myriad product forms and endeared itself into our hearts, and stomachs as well.

[Executive, India]

Havaianas

A plastic sandal that costs $3 [US] a pair and is one of the most popular and loved brands in Brazil. Everybody has a pair of Havaianas–the poorest Brazilian as well as the richest one. And the mystery about this brand is that the richer the consumer is, the more he likes the brand.

[Consultant, Brazil]

The New Yorker

A belletrist safe house for those craving word, wit, and smart cultural commentary (and sometimes just shameless gossip!). The cartoons are like the best Woody Allen moments; student dorms everywhere owe Saul Steinberg for interiors. Its contents page actually means it. It takes itself seriously, but isn't afraid to go fancy dress or be seen in glasses. It's got a permanent parking space on the magazine rack. It's what you want to find under the coffee table while backpacking through Thailand or stuck in a hotel. It's unquestionably NYC, but you wish this was YOUR local rag.

[Writer, New Zealand]

Vigelandsparken

The biggest park in Oslo, Norway, is more than trees, lawns, and awesome statues by Gustav Vigeland. It's love. Love for summer, fall, winter, and spring, love for nature, changing colors throughout the year, love for children, dogs, and tourists with cameras, as well as for barbequing, football, Frisbees, and the way Norwegians enjoy the summer like nobody else, just smiling even more as they're playing in the snow.

[Mechanic, Norway]

Trung Nguyen

Vietnam's equivalent to Starbucks, Trung Nguyen is a chain of cafes that sells great Vietnamese coffee in a comfortable, relaxed environment. Besides the quality of the coffee and environment, people love them because they are local!

[Entrepreneur, Vietnam]

Fado

Fado is a very typical music of Portugal, that perfectly expresses the reality of Portuguese emotions. It speaks with a quiet dignity born of the realization that any mortal desire or plan is at risk of destruction by powers beyond individual control.

[TV producer, Portugal]

Superman

My bond with this fictional character goes far beyond mere childhood joy at his colorful adventures printed on the cheapest of paper. Superman is the almost-messianic tale of an only son sent from the heavens by his father to help the mortals of Earth. Superman is the unique (and downright twisted) two-sided, romantic triangle of mild-mannered Clark Kent battling his own dazzling alter-ego to win the heart of Lois Lane…the enduring creation of two Depression-era Jewish teens from Cleveland, Ohio… and every bit the never-ending battle of Christopher Reeve to rise and walk again. Superman taught me how to read, how to appreciate art, and how to dream. To this day, the four-color icon inspires people to set their sights a little higher and look…up in the sky….

[Credit controller, U.S.A.]

42 Below

The classy tall-neck. The vodka from Aotearoa New Zealand that's all about location, location, location. Produced where the chilled Antarctic currents meet the sultry Pacific. Fresh, cool and warm down the throat when you're agape to the pure air. And of course its best imbibed there: I'm a fall-guy for the feijoa-infused edition–tart, crisp, taste-of-the-local, (solo or mixed with crushed ice, fresh lime, and ginger beer) drunk outside on a breezy spring day, Fat Freddy's beats going down with it, watching the clouds scud under the Southern Cross. Choice!

[Barman, U.K.]

The Statue of the Virgin Mary, Harissa

This gigantic statue of the Virgin Mary has been a symbol of Lebanon for more than 50 years, having stood perched on a mountain overlooking the sea since 1908. It was always cloaked in a sense of mystery. During war days, thousands swore that the statue moved and protected the houses from missiles with its hands. This statue has such high respect with many visitors, including Muslims, who flock to it each year, going around its steps to see Lebanon from Mary's eyes.

[Account director, Lebanon]

XXXX

Queensland, where this beer is brewed, has a name for being one of the hottest and least civilized places in far north Australia. They say that XXXX beer got its name because Queenslanders couldn't spell beer. I think there just aren't enough letters in the alphabet to come up with a word that describes the taste of XXXX beer at the end of a hot day's work. It's like liquid gold when you're thirsty. Queenslanders love their beer, because in a place where one of the kids' first words is "drought," it washes down the dust and quenches our thirst like no other brew.

[Graphic designer, Australia]

Yorkshire Pudding

What's your favorite meal, I ask? It's a full Sunday Roast! And what's the best part of that meal? The one thing that people fight for more of? It's the Yorkshire Pudding. It's simple. The best of the best. The most loved of the most loved. (In memory of Nan.)

[Student, U.K.]

Contents

Foreword
by A.G. Lafley, Chairman, President, and Chief Executive, The Procter & Gamble Company

The best brands consistently win two crucial moments of truth. The first moment occurs at the store shelf, when a consumer decides whether to buy one brand or another. The second occurs at home, when she uses the brand—and is delighted, or isn't. Brands that win these moments of truth again and again earn a special place in consumers' hearts and minds; the strongest of these establish a lifelong bond with consumers.

Most of the fastest-growing P&G brands today focus intensely on winning these moments of truth. They are in touch with consumers, not as demographics or psychographics, but as people—as individuals. Fast-growing brands such as Crest, Olay, and Pampers have very emotional, aspirational equities. We are learning that a brand like Crest doesn't stand only for toothpaste or toothbrushes, but for healthy smiles—and an expanding lineup of branded products and services that can help create those smiles.

It's no coincidence that all of these brands are growing with the help of Kevin Roberts and his colleagues at Saatchi & Saatchi. I've known and have worked closely with Kevin for seven years. His passionate belief in building brands consumers love is inspirational, and effective. It is helping reinvent how we at P&G think about creating, nurturing, and growing big brands.

This book will provide even the most experienced marketers with fresh new ways to think about branding. It provokes readers to think about mystery, sensuality, and intimacy as brand-building tools. It provides practical insights into leveraging the power of emotion, respect, and love. And it provides proven case studies that bring the Lovemark concept to life.

In short, this is an important book for all of us who care about consumers and the brands they love.

A.G. Lafley, Chairman, President, and Chief Executive,
The Procter & Gamble Company

For Enyd and Rita

Two Lovemarks of mine

Chapter 1

START ME UP

I was born an optimist.

I always looked for opportunities where others faced up to threats or weaknesses. I believed if you were going through hell the only option was to keep going!

During my childhood in Lancaster I always believed that nothing was impossible. Where better to find myself than as CEO Worldwide of Saatchi & Saatchi, the Ideas Company that made this belief a founding declaration?

I've been lucky to have been guided by exceptional people who have mentored me. Inspirational Players. People who believe that to dream is as important as to act, and that winners are powered by passion and emotion.

By the time I was ready to enter the world of work I wanted to go somewhere that was top of its class. Somewhere that relied on passion and inspiration as its driving force. Who better to work for than the most inspirational businesswoman of the 60s, Mary Quant?

Mary opened her famous London boutique Bazaar in 1955 and was swinging-60s London personified. The miniskirts, hot-pants, shiny plastic raincoats, and paint-box makeup all added up to the Mary Quant decade. Mary was the first person to operationalize the concept "less is more." As she said:

"A woman is only as young as her knees."

When Beatle George Harrison and model Patti Boyd married in 1966, they both dressed head-to-toe in Quant.

By the time I arrived in 1969, the Mary Quant brand was expanding into a very hot international business. They were still riding high on Mary's 1967 whimsy: "Good taste is death. Vulgarity is life." In my early 20s, what more could I ask for?

It wasn't my incredible cool and fashion sense that landed me the job. It was because I had learned French and Spanish at school and Quant was moving into Europe. As one does, I started in the lowest of jobs: Assistant Brand Manager. The business was moving so fast it wasn't long before they promoted my marketing manager and a gaping opportunity opened up right in front of me.

I went to Tony Evans, the boss of the international division, and said,

"I'll do the job for half the salary of the previous guy for the next six months. If you think I'm worth it, then you can pay me what the job deserves."

He said, "Okay, you're on. Do it."

Working in cosmetics was incredible. Everything happened so fast. It was try, fail, learn, try again, win, try again. Every month. We were growing our business at 500 percent a year with a product lifecycle of around nine months. That's new products conceived, launched, sold, and discontinued within nine months!

For me it was like enrolling in the University of Branding. I loved every minute. Innovation and fun were our passion. We were the first to do "makeup to make love in": a waterproof kissable lipstick, waterproof mascara. We did the first ever makeup for men.

With her perfectly on-brand, super cool haircut by Vidal Sassoon, Mary understood as well as anyone I have ever met that brands are about emotion and personality. She also knew that in the end it was what consumers desired that would propel her business into the stratosphere. "The fundamentals of fashion remain the same," she wrote in her book, *Quant by Quant*:

"Women wear clothes to make them feel good and to feel sexy. Women turn themselves on. Men like to look at women to be turned on–to feel sexy is to know you're alive."

Whenever I am in meetings and hear complicated strategies for getting consumer attention, I remember Mary Quant's simple belief in human desires and passions.

My experience in bringing new products to market landed me my next job: Gillette's International New Products Manager for their fast-growing business in the Middle East. It was my first taste of the serious corporate world; a three-year stay where I first visited the Casino du Liban, flew Pan Am 001, and started a love affair with Gillette razor blades that grows stronger with every innovation they launch. I'm now a Mach 3 Turbo junkie. Gillette was the first step towards the company that would change my life: Procter & Gamble, the international multi-billion-dollar consumer goods company. The people who invented brand management.

My relationship with P&G started on January 1, 1975–the day I joined. What can I say? I love P&G. I always have.

I found out everything important I know about people, business, and marketing at P&G.

And in amazing places like Sana'a, Al Ain, Casablanca, and Felixstowe Ferry where I spent five months selling P&G brands to the trade. I love P&G's scale. I love the ambition of the enterprise. The disciplines invented at P&G have shaped my life. To be a P&G Brand Manager in the 1970s was to be King of the World.

In the Middle East I learned lessons that have been invaluable to me about how to connect with consumers, and how to do it in a place where mass marketing was in its infancy.

I learned to love the people. In Arab countries you make friends for life. The people were genuine, emotional, family-focused, hospitable. They understood their traditions and the past, and they really understood that they had a completely different future. It was very exciting. There was little resistance to the new because they didn't have much of a present. They had a past and they had a future.

I also learned there that you could make a big difference fast. There weren't Western-style barriers in place, so new ideas got to the surface much quicker. There was no bureaucracy to go through, they didn't have an organized, data-rich trade to say "NO!" And you didn't have corporate HQ on your tail. When you brought Tide, Ariel, or Pampers into Oujda, Abha, or Salalah it was truly life-changing. It didn't improve lives a little bit: it improved lives significantly.

P&G is a company totally committed to doing the right thing. Why?

Because the principles don't belong to Procter & Gamble, they belong to the people who work there.

John Pepper, Herbert Schmitz, Ron Pearce, and Fouad Kuryatim live the principles–and the dreams–every day. No one lives these values more than current P&G leader A.G. Lafley.

All these years later I still believe in the power of those principles I learned at P&G. Totally. Charles Decker summed up many of the best in his book, *Winning with the P&G 99*. Do the right thing. Capitalize on your mistakes. Winning is everything. Think sideways. Make something happen. Never try to fool the consumer.

For me the Middle East was perfect. It was full of adventure and I could be out there in the streets and markets, watching, listening, doing, learning. Seven years later, still in love with the Middle East, I seized an opportunity and moved to another great company–Pepsi. More fantastic opportunities and serious challenges. Like building a Pepsi plant in Kathmandu. Like graduating from Pepsi's elite negotiation school and getting "the Iraq job" on the strength of it. Like building seven Pepsi plants in Iraq.

Pepsi introduced me to more Inspirational Players like Roger Enrico, Alan Pottasch–the father of the Pepsi generation–and a tough nut with a heart of gold, Bob Beeby–President of PepsiCo International.

I became President and CEO of Pepsi in Canada in 1987. Another world! In the Middle East, Pepsi was Number One; in Canada it was a different story. We had been sitting behind Coke for years. If you want to learn about the power of brands at street level, the Pepsi/Coke battle is as good a place as any I know. In Canada we had the added problem of competing against some of Pepsi's own brands like Diet Pepsi and Mountain Dew. So Pepsi itself was at risk of sliding to Number Three, don't worry about Number Two.

My gut reaction has always been to zig when everyone else zags. The best way for us to avoid becoming Number Three, I figured, was to become Number One!

Lemonade was a really big category in Canada. So we bought the 7 UP brand. At the same time we drove Diet Pepsi hard against Diet Coke, the independent bottlers' network took up the challenge and street by street, city by city, province by province, just poured it on. We passed Coke. Nothing is impossible.

At that time, in the late 1980s, Canada was anxious about the implications of the Free Trade Agreement with the United States, and how it was going to be the end of all things Canadian. I took the completely opposite view. My feeling was that because Canada was small, fast, and flexible, we couldn't lose.

Being on the edge of the United States made us more powerful, not less. Great things always come from the edge, as I've had the chance to discover personally.

To inspire our people and partners, we hired a very big and very smart hotel in Toronto. Everyone came: the trade, our own people, all our bottlers, the media. My keynote speech was all about competition. How Pepsi had just beaten Coke, and how, in the same way, Canada could be competitive with America. About halfway through my presentation, a huge red-and-white Coca-Cola vending machine rolled onto the stage. I ignored it.

As I ended my speech I reached down behind the podium, picked up a machine gun and started blasting the Coke dispenser.

When you machine-gun a vending machine, it makes a serious noise.

We had people diving under tables and heading for the doors. It was incredible. For safety's sake we had involved the Royal Canadian Mounted Police, so we weren't being completely irresponsible.

And what happened the next day? The word around the trade was unbelievable. The shoot-up was on the news, in the papers and magazines. It was the power of humor and branding at work in very different times. And it truly galvanized our sales force and our bottlers.

The edge gives us a special attitude. Cutting edge, leading edge, bleeding edge, the edge

and extreme. Great ideas can come from anywhere, but most of them turn up on the edge.

Great ideas, like humor, come from the corners of the mind, out on the edge. That's why humor can break up log-jams in both personal relationships and in business.

I have always loved the extreme, and my next move proved it. I went from Canada, a large continent at the top of the world, to an extraordinary country on the very edge of the Pacific Ocean–New Zealand. In 1989 I moved to Auckland with my family as Chief Operating Officer for Lion Nathan, which was led by Douglas Myers (another Inspirational Player).

The first time I met with the financial analysts at Lion Nathan in New Zealand, I walked into the room with a real lion I had borrowed from the zoo. I can tell you, from that day on, no one in the company ever forgot the Lion in Lion Nathan!

Over the next seven years we transformed Lion Nathan from a large New Zealand brewer to a significant force in the Asia-Pacific beverage industry. And I transformed my life as well.

Having worked on most continents and in many, many countries, I found my place in these upside-down islands. Not that I spent all my time there, even then. In the early 1990s I became a huge China fan. I am to this day. I spent a lot of time in China for Lion Nathan researching market and investment opportunities. We built a brand new $150 million brewery in Suzhou, the most advanced brewing operation in China. And I got to experience the pleasures of local brands of beer. We also moved our Asian HQ from Hong Kong to Shanghai.

My home is New Zealand. We're as close to the South Pole as you can get and still have running water. The edge gives us a special attitude. Cutting edge, leading edge, bleeding edge, the edge of inspiration, on the edge of our seats. It's a place to shake off conventions and worn-out formulas, and shake out ideas. New ideas. The edge is exciting and risky and extreme. I love it.

I believe "edge cultures" will have even higher value in this millennium. Great ideas can come from anywhere, but most of them turn up on the edge. The places that are restless and resourceful. The places that don't understand "can't be done."

of inspiration, on the edge of our seats. The edge is exciting and risky

Why did I find the idea of working in a seemingly isolated country like New Zealand so compelling? For a start, it's seductive and extreme. It's about freedom from orthodoxy and conformity. It's about exciting new ideas, interesting people unconstrained by the need to conform to the mores of New York or London.

The power of the edge is one of today's most compelling ideas.

It is based on a biological metaphor and, to my mind, will have a dramatic effect on the way we all think about change.

When species change, it almost always occurs first at the fringes. Here the population is most sparse and the orthodoxies of the center are weakest. Here you can flourish isolated from formula and rules, free from the corrosive belief that everything great has already been done.

NOTHING IS IMPOSSIBLE

To be revered as a hothouse

for world-changing creative

ideas that transform

our clients' brands,

businesses and

reputations.

I signed up on the spot. Saatchi & Saatchi gave me the chance to test my belief in the power of big ideas and in emotion.

I was determined to refocus on emotional connections, both within Saatchi & Saatchi and with people everywhere. There was pressure on me to restructure the business. We're talking 1997, when the management consultancies were still in the ascendancy with their slice 'n' dice recipe for dealing with anything that moved. I was advised to bring in my trusted guys: my HR guy, my marketing guy, my money guy. Instead I brought in nobody and I moved nobody for two years.

My instinct was to go against the prevailing wisdom. I went to Saatchi & Saatchi people and said, "Here's our Inspirational Dream. We're all going to pull together to stay in the premier league for 24 months. After that, we'll think about making changes, bringing people in and moving people around. I think you can do it, and we're all going to do this thing together." As it turned out, they could. And we did.

In my experience, when you go into most companies what you find is good people and bad management. You can turn that around really quickly by starting with an Inspirational Dream, setting some challenges, and getting everybody focused.

As it worked out, to get moving took only one year, not ten, as one wise-guy predicted.

And in that time we were also able to kick-start three great ideas.

The first
was to transform Saatchi & Saatchi from an advertising agency into an Ideas Company.
In fact, the hottest Ideas Company on the planet.

The second
was to start delivering not just great performance, but Peak Performance.
Saatchi & Saatchi had to be Number One, Two, or Three in the world–preferably Number One.
We had to be in continuous contention–and we would do it with inspiration.

And the third
was the most exciting of them all. It combined everything I had learned.
It was the answer to the critical question:

What comes after brands?

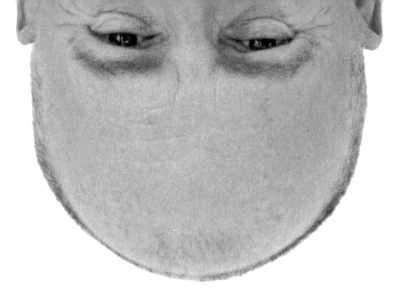

For more years than I can remember I have used the same shampoo: Head & Shoulders. Ridiculous, isn't it? I mean it's a shampoo to remove dandruff, which it does. But I've no hair, let alone dandruff! Still, I love Head & Shoulders. I won't buy or use anything else.

It's a Lovemark of mine.

Chapter 2

TIME CHANGES
EVERYTHING

Over the years, I have visited China many times. Saatchi & Saatchi was one of the first businesses to take part in China's amazing transformation. It has been nothing short of awe-inspiring to watch this enormously complex and ancient nation assimilate Western business practices in a matter of a few years. And set out to surpass them.

The Chinese have an ancient curse: "May you live in interesting times." Well, my message to China is:

Hold on to your hats, interesting times ahead.

Not only is China borrowing from the powerful financial and social models of the West, but they are doing it at a time when those very models are shifting fundamentally.

The journey from products to trademarks to brands is one of the great stories of the last century. It is a story that has had profound effects on how businesses deal with consumers. And how people deal with businesses.

Each step has brought consumers closer to the businesses that produce the goods and services they need. Closer to their need for design, quality, price, usability, availability, innovation, and safety.

Each step has:

- turned up the voice of the consumer
- added weight to what is most difficult to measure—the intangibles of relationships, brands...people power
- pulled emotion closer to the center

Interesting times? I love them.

Products to trademarks

In the beginning, products were just, well…products. One product was pretty much indistinguishable from another. Get hit over the head with Jake's club or Fred's club, the headache was much the same. Trade was kept in the family. Making the right choice was easy.

But people being people, even in such a simple trading system, trademarks made an early entry. There are trademarks on pottery in Mesopotamia (now Iraq) dating as far back as 3,000 B.C.

There is a cafe I go to named SPQR. It is named after one of the most feared and respected trademarks the world has ever known. Four letters that told you the mighty Roman Empire was at hand.

Over the centuries, trade increasingly stretched past local boundaries and the importance of trademarks increased. Fine to trust the local village blacksmith. You could check out the forge, bite the metal, ask around. But the weird guy bringing in iron implements from the next village? Not so easy. So trademarks moved up a notch from simple name-tags to marks of trust and reliability.

From a business perspective, trademarks play great defense. They offer legal protection for the unique qualities of your products and services, and declare your interests. Trademarks define territory. That's how it works when you are in charge of a business.

To consumers, the picture looks somewhat different.

Consumers care about a trademark because it offers reassurance. "This will have the quality I paid for."

For both sides, businesses and consumers, trademarks are a sign of continuity in a constantly shifting environment.

As Kate Wilson, a prominent New Zealand patent attorney, once told me:

"Patents expire, copyrights eventually run their course, but trademarks last forever."

Trademarks are not exempt from change. SPQR gets thousands of hits on Google, but most of them are not for the Senate and People of Rome but for a popular computer game–*SPQR: The Empire's Darkest Hour*!

The history of trademarks is littered with once-famous names that have gone generic. Bad news for them, as all the value they have created with consumers can be sucked up by just about anyone. Band-Aid has become the generic term for any bandage that sticks over a small wound. Jell-O and Vaseline have been pushed down the same route. And the process is still happening. In some countries, unique product names like Rollerblades and Walkman have been accepted as the given and defining names for in-line skates and portable music players.

Just holding a trademark doesn't guarantee successful differentiation, but it can be a great start. Over the 20th century some trademarks have grown into enduring icons.

The MGM lion first roared in 1928 for the silent movie *White Shadows of the South Seas*. Work out the technology on that one! And if you have ever wondered what it says in the circle that frames the lion, try *Ars Gratia Artis*–Art for Art's Sake.

The classic Coca-Cola bottle was designed in 1915 and registered as a trademark in 1960. Even the stories around the bottle design are great, with lots of mysterious connections. Reminds me of the urban myths around the clubbers' energy drink Red Bull. Contains bull semen. Secret weapon the military canned. Etcetera, etcetera.

"The most perfectly designed package in the world."

[Raymond Loewy]

The letters IBM are one of the great trademarks of the 20th century. So protective was the company of its high status that when Stanley Kubrick wanted to use an IBM machine as the rogue computer in *2001: A Space Odyssey*, the company pulled out. Kubrick, tongue-in-cheek, named the soft-spoken killer computer by moving one letter back in the alphabet, and creating HAL.

In an average day you can expect to have contact with around 1,500 trademarked products. If you go to the supermarket, rack that up to 35,000!

Everyone wants to trademark their stuff. Names and slogans are old hat. Now the push is to trademark shapes, scents, and sounds. Even colors.

Owens Corning trademarked the very particular PINK® of their fiberglass insulation material in the 1980s.

THIS IS NOT "CORNING PINK"

But not all expansionary efforts have been successful. In June of 2000, Harley-Davidson finally gave up its gutsy six-year effort to trademark the roar of its V-Twin engine. In its application, the company claimed that the sound of this engine was "as recognizable to motorcycle enthusiasts as 'The Star Spangled Banner.'"

Other manufacturers fought this claim hard. They knew how much the sexy roar meant to middle-aged bikers and they couldn't let Harley own it.

Harley-Davidson finally withdrew.

Joanne Bischmann, the company's Vice President of Marketing, said, "If our customers know the sound cannot be imitated, that's good enough for me and for Harley-Davidson."

TRADEMARKS & BRANDS

The idea of separating one product from another with the aid of trademarks was a good one. And it worked–for a while. That was until it came up against business' own *necrotizing fasciitis*, or flesh-eating disease: commodification.

For anyone in business, the rapid cycling of their valued products into generic stuff is a dark and constant fear.

One day you are sitting on a premium product, enjoying high margins and fighting off consumers. The next your product is being bottom-loaded on back shelves or dumped into "Specials" bins.

The warning signs:

Consistent

Abundant

Interchangeable

Impersonal

Homogenous

Lowest Price

Now we're not just talking about bulk stuff like salt and pork bellies, rice and sugar. Anything can become a commodity, given enough competitive pressure. Consider the once mighty airline industry. No wonder brands were seized on as a way to fight back.

Brands were developed to create differences for products that were in danger of becoming as hard to tell apart as chunks of gravel.

They are also a proven way for companies to capture and exploit their innovations. If you are making a big R&D investment you are going to protect it with a patent. But the little ™ or "patent pending" note was never enough. You had to make sure everyone knows the value of what they are getting. Brands do this brilliantly.

When I was working with Procter & Gamble in the 1970s, we were proud that it was P&G that had articulated the concept of brands first. Neil McElroy was a hero. He had understood the potential of the brand idea and codified it in 1931 into the brand-management system that made it a reality.

P&G understood that brand disciplines could bring together the legal protection of patents and trademarks with the stuff that has meaning for consumers: consistency, quality, performance, and value.

Commodities got a big hit, right on the nose.

They wouldn't be back for another round until late in the century.

Our world of brands

As we watch television, open the mail, or go for a stroll, we now live in a world of brands.

My experience on the street–in the back offices of retailers and at bottling plants as we battled for Pepsi in the Middle East–gave me the first hints that branding was at the final frontier.

Talking with consumers, I could see that as their choices grew wider, their loyalty to brands that didn't touch them in any personal way was shaky.

And there was much more competition coming. Sure the main event was the tussle between us and Coke, but more and more local and international competition was edging in.

The deep insight for me was that many of our marketers saw Pepsi as a business of margins. This is the first sure step towards becoming a commodity. I always thought of Pepsi's business as a business of selling case by case. Let me explain.

One of the realities I faced in business was that I didn't have an M.B.A. I hadn't been trained in all the rules–so it meant I had to focus on the people: they were the ones who did the real day-to-day business and were close to consumers.

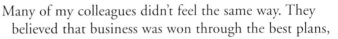

Many of my colleagues didn't feel the same way. They believed that business was won through the best plans, memos, recommendations, and position papers. I believed that the cola business was won through cases. Individual cases of Pepsi sold by individual retailers to individual people who wanted to drink it.

Cases are strategic. Herbert Schmitz at P&G told me that. He was right. And because I believed this, and still believe it to this day, I was never in the office. I'm still not.

Later, when I was working for Lion Nathan and marketing beer, the fundamental problems with brands became even clearer. There is no such thing as bad beer. They're all refreshing, taste great, and are the world's best social lubricant. Technology is not a barrier. Beer is really still just a local cottage industry. Breweries are everywhere.

Through the lens of this incredibly competitive business I could see a relentless process that was turning what we truly valued into the commonplace.

To me it was clear that brands were stuck on the "-er" words: Bigger, brighter, better, stronger, faster, easier, newer and, the final stake through the heart, cheaper. These are all tablestakes, just the stake any player has to bring to the game to earn a seat at the table. I remember seeing a cover article in *The Economist*. It declared that 1988 was "The Year of the Brand." I thought, "Yeah, right. But is it the beginning or the end?"

The Attention Economy

Brands had a dream-run pumping the global economy. Maybe they could have survived the pressures of commodification if not for one big and unavoidable fact. By the 1990s it was clear that we were living in the Attention Economy. There were thousands of TV channels, movies, radio stations, newspapers, and magazines. Millions of websites. Billions of phone calls, faxes, and e-mails. And right through all of it, new product launches and new improved product-line extensions and ads struggling to be heard. Too much information!

People are overwhelmed by the choices they face. Forget the Information Economy. Human attention has become our principal currency.

"I don't want 500 television channels. I just want the one channel that gives me what I want to see."

[Nicholas Negroponte, MIT Media Lab]

Job Number One for any marketer these days is competing for attention. Whoever you are. Wherever you are. And once you've captured that attention, you've got to show you deserve it.

The process really only has two steps—so why does everyone find it so hard? It's all because we obsess over the attention part and forget about why we need that attention in the first place: the relationships.

Emotional connections with consumers have to be at the foundation of all our cool marketing moves and innovative tactics. Viral marketing, guerrilla marketing, entertainment marketing, experience marketing—they can all seize attention if they are done right, but once they have it, they have nowhere much to put it. Nothing to build, nothing to add to, nothing to value or care about.

Let the telemarketing debacle be a warning. When it was first hot in the 1980s it was a raging success. You could sell ANYTHING on the phone. Fast-forward a decade or so and you looked at a very different picture.

Even if the telemarketers get past our answering machines and caller ID, the rules have changed dramatically. Nowadays we'll hang up rather than order the steak knives.

Brands are out of juice...

They can't stand out in the marketplace, and they are struggling to connect with people. Here are six reasons why:

1. Brands are worn out from overuse

Michael Eisner of Disney has called the word brand "overused, sterile, and unimaginative." He's right. As the brand manual grows heavier and more detailed, you know you're in trouble. Making sure the flowers in reception conform to the brand guidelines just shows you are looking in the wrong direction. Consumers are who you should be paying attention to. What matters to them. Otherwise, you're hiding, and you're in trouble.

2. Brands are no longer mysterious

There is a new anti-brand sensibility. There is much more consumer awareness, more consumers who understand how brands work and, more importantly, how brands are intended to work on them! For most brands, there is nowhere left to hide. The information age means that brands are part of the public domain. Hidden agendas, subliminal messages, tricky moves…forget it. For most brands, it is a new age of consumer savvy; at the extremes, it's the attacks of Naomi Klein and the anti-global gang.

3. Brands can't understand the new consumer

The new consumer is better informed, more critical, less loyal, and harder to read. The white suburban housewife who for decades seemed to buy all the soap powder no longer exists. She has been joined by a new population of multi-generational, multi-ethnic, multi-national consumers.

4. Brands struggle with good old-fashioned competition

The more brands we invent, the less we notice them as individuals. If you're not Number One or Two, you might as well forget it. And the greater the number of brands, the thinner the resources promoting them. You get a treadmill of novelty, production value, incremental change, tactical promotions, and events.

5. Brands have been captured by formula

I lose patience with the wanna-be science of brands. The definitions, the charts, tables, and diagrams. There are too many people following the same rule book. When everybody tries to beat differentiation in the same way, nobody gets anywhere. You get row upon row of what I call "brandroids." Formulas can't deal with human emotion. Formulas have no imagination or empathy.

6. Brands have been smothered by creeping conservatism

The story of brands has gone from daring and inspiration to caution and risk-aversion. Once the darling of the bold and the brave, brands are relying on the accumulation of past experiences rather than the potential of future ones. Headstones are replacing stepping stones. If the antics of Richard Branson cause a riot (and they do), how bland and boring has everyone else become?

Brands can no longer cope with some of the most important challenges we face today as marketers, producers, traders, and business people.

- How to cut through the information clutter
- How to connect meaningfully with consumers
- How to create integrated experiences
- How to convince people to commit for life
- How to make the world a better place

There is only one way to thrive as marketers in the Attention Economy:

Stop racing after every new fad and focus on making consistent, emotional connections with consumers. If you stand for nothing, you fall for everything.

The journey is over

The great journey from products to trademarks and from trademarks to brands is over. Trademarks are tablestakes. Brands are tablestakes. Both are useful in the quest for differentiation and vital to survival, but they're not winning game-breakers.

Today the stakes have reached a new high. The social fabric is spread more thinly than ever. People are looking for new, emotional connections. They are looking for what they can love. They are insisting on more choice, they have higher expectations, and they need emotional pull to help them make decisions. And, finally, they want more ways to connect with everything in their lives–including brands.

Businesses have always assumed that people see the brands the same way they do. This is why they can get it SO-O-O-O wrong.

But some special brands don't seem to make that mistake. They are so far out in front that they seem to have evolved into something else. They are what inspired Saatchi & Saatchi to develop Lovemarks as the future beyond brands.

Chapter 3

EMOTIONAL
RESCUE

In my 35 years in business I have always trusted my emotions. I have always believed that by touching emotion you get the best people to work with you, the best clients to inspire you, the best partners, and the most devoted customers.

The last ten years have seen emotion dominate the bestseller—and the not-so-bestseller—lists. Click your way through Amazon.com for titles and see what I mean. *Art and Emotion*, *Body and Emotion*, *Culture and Emotion*, *Reason and Emotion*. Sounds fine. Then there's *Emotion and Spirit*, *Emotion and Focus*, *Emotion and Religion*, *Emotion and Insanity*, *Emotion in Organizations*. There's more where that came from.

People everywhere are wa

Emotion has become a legitimate subject for serious research. Onc● what was obvious to everyone who cared to look.

In the business world there's *Emotional Branding, Emotional Markets, Emotional Capital, Emotional Value* and, of course, *Emotional Marketing* from my friends at Hallmark.

It goes deeper. How about *Emotional Intelligence, Emotional Genius, Emotional Unavailability*. And then, a little further out in the galaxy, *Emotional Yoga, Emotional Cleansing, Emotional Alchemy, Emotional Claustrophobia*, and *Emotional Control*.

And two books no self-respecting business should be without; the helpful *Emotionally Weird*, and the essential *Emotional Vampires*.

...nting to embrace emotion.

...he scientists got into emotion it didn't take them long to prove

"Father and Son"

Cat Stevens was a mega-star of the 1970s with such hits to his credit as "Moonshadow," "Morning Has Broken," and "Peace Train." He converted to Islam in 1977, changed his name to Yusuf Islam, and pretty well left the music business. Since then, he has devoted his time to charities and education in support of his religion. He is very cautious about the use of his music. Many of his songs deal with themes from his life before conversion, and he no longer wants to be associated with them. Little surprise then that he had never allowed any of his songs to be used in TV commercials.

When creatives at Saatchi & Saatchi Wellington got it into their heads to use a Cat Stevens song for a commercial, the first reaction was "find another song." Trouble was, the song they wanted was absolutely perfect: "Father and Son."

I was once like you are now,
and I know that it's not easy
to be calm when you've found something going on.
But take your time, think a lot,
why, think of everything you've got.
For you will still be here tomorrow,
but your dreams may not.

Our people didn't just want the song as the background music. The song was the story. An emotional portrait of a most special relationship–a father and son growing together from birth to death.

The client was Telecom New Zealand. Like many other telecommunications companies, they had never been big on emotion. They are under intense pressure every minute of every day. The whole industry lives in a waking nightmare of margin-shaving, competition, unexpected technology shifts, rising consumer expectations. They usually don't see people's feelings as a priority.

But Telecom New Zealand had been a monopoly and was now confronting competition with energy. They were adventurous and up for a challenge. They knew that when you act like a commodity, you get treated like one–that old vicious cycle. Forget about being loved; it's tough to get even a little respect on the street.

That might have been the end of the story in some places, but our people took it as a personal challenge. They truly believe that Nothing is Impossible. A passionate plea to Yusuf was drafted. Sure, permission had never been given before, but that was then. Our people pinned their hearts to their letter and waited. Weeks later as the team sat in the mixing room despairing of even getting a response, they heard the rustle of a fax. It was from Yusuf. He had responded to the visuals accompanying his words and the emotional truth of the story. He had written one word on the fax they had sent him pleading to use his song: "Yes."

Since joining Saatchi & Saatchi, I have given hundreds of presentations around the globe. "Father and Son" is the spot I always play at the end.

In Dubai, Denmark, Los Angeles, London, New York, São Paulo, Barcelona, and Sydney, the response never varies. People feel this spot is talking to them personally. The story makes a deep emotional connection.

Our client wanted a more connected country– Cat Stevens sang the song. His Greatest Hits album moved into the Top 10 CD sales in New Zealand a month after launch.

Human beings are powered by emotion, not by reason

Study after study has proven that if the emotion centers of our brain are damaged in some way, we don't just lose the ability to laugh or cry, we lose the ability to make decisions. Alarm bells for every business right there.

The neurologist Donald Calne puts it brilliantly:

"The essential difference between emotion and reason is that emotion leads to action while reason leads to conclusions."

You don't have to be a brain surgeon to get that. The reality we face does not require mastery of arcane terminology, and it's not about evaluating competing theories about how the mind works or how it is structured.

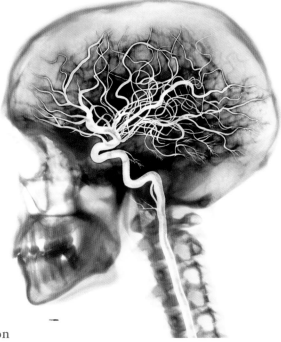

The brain is more complex, more densely connected, and more mysterious than any of us can dream. That's as much as we have to know. Emotion and reason are intertwined, but when they are in conflict, emotion wins every time. Without the fleeting and intense stimulus of emotion, rational thought winds down and disintegrates.

Maurice Lévy, Chairman of Publicis Groupe, owners of Saatchi & Saatchi, elaborates:

"Consumers who make decisions based purely on facts represent a very small minority of the world's population. They are people without feelings, or perhaps people who put their heart and emotions in the fridge when they are leaving home in the morning, and only take them out again when they go back home in the evening. Although even for these people, there is always some product or service they buy based on impulse or emotion.

"The vast majority of the population, however, consumes *and* shops with their mind and their heart, or if you prefer, their emotions. They look for a rational reason: what the product does and why it is a superior choice. And they take an emotional decision: I like it, I prefer it, I feel good about it.

"The way this works is very subtle. Most of the time, before seeing something in detail, you have a sense of what it is. Before understanding, you feel. And making people feel good about a brand, getting a positive emotion, is key. This is what makes the difference.

"To get emotion back into business in this period when cost-cutting is king is very difficult. People making decisions are tense, under pressure, and rationality is reassuring. But emotions are more rewarding, both in the short and long-term."

[Maurice Lévy, Chairman, Publicis Groupe, Paris]

Writer Virginia Postrel has a great example of how ignoring the real emotions of consumers can point us in the wrong direction. About ten years ago, many women's fashion retailers had the same dumb idea: it's possible to rationally predict what women want. The demographics said that women were getting older and bigger and so perfect logic kicked in. Older, bigger women are not going to be interested in youth, novelty, or sex appeal. Bad call. Turned out that women didn't feel older and bigger at all. They rushed to buy slinky slip-dresses and curvy, miniskirted business suits. The logicians tanked and the few retailers who backed a genuine understanding of the human heart did great.

What is important is to engage with the new realities of emotion. We must work out what they mean to us. How they affect behavior. And then do something different because of it. Marketing people *talk* about emotion. They present charts and diagrams, even raise their voices and wave their arms, but fundamentally they treat emotion as…out-there, felt by someone else and able to be manipulated.

Analyzing other people's emotions and refusing to acknowledge our own dumps us in the same old rut. What a waste. The emotions are a serious opportunity to get in touch with consumers. And best of all, emotion is an unlimited resource. It's always there–waiting to be tapped with new ideas, new inspirations, new experiences.

So what kind of emotions are we talking about? Everyone has a different list, but people tend to agree on two points: first, emotions can be separated into primary and secondary emotions; and second, most of our emotions are negative. Emotions can inspire and excite us. They can also frighten and threaten us. It's survival. Our emotions tell us what's important, and in our ancient past it was smart to pay the most attention to the bad stuff.

Primary emotions are brief, intense, and they cannot be controlled. I'd join emotion researcher Dylan Evans of King's College London and go for:

Joy
Sorrow
Anger
Fear
Surprise
Disgust

To me what is really striking about the secondary emotions is how social they are. And how important they are. You can feel primary emotions when you are alone. But to work up a secondary emotion you need someone else around. These so-called secondary emotions are not secondary in reality. They make up the volatile mix from which human relationships are formed, which makes them pretty fundamental.

As for those more complex secondary emotions that combine the head with the heart, let's agree on:

Love
Guilt
Shame
Pride
Envy
Jealousy

Which brings us right to Emotion Number One. The most fundamental of them all...

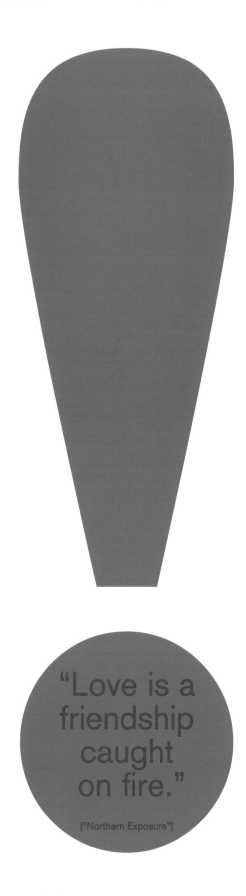

"Love is a
friendship
caught
on fire."

["Northern Exposure"]

Chapter 4

ALL
YOU
NEED
IS
LOVE

My late father-in-law Don Honeywill played the famous sax intro on the Beatles song "All You Need Is Love." It's a song that means a lot to me and my family. Intimacy in action.

Plato got it right: "At the touch of Love, everyone becomes a poet." Or a cynic. I'm no cynic. At Saatchi & Saatchi our pursuit of Love and what it could mean for business has been focused and intense. People love people. We love experiences, we love teams, we love events, we love abstract ideas like our country or town or cause. We love art. And we love stuff. The objects we make or buy or exchange. The objects that define who we are and where we stand.

We are consumers by nature. For virtually all the world's citizens, our possessions add meaning to our lives. That's why we buy, exchange, give, treasure, and possess them.

The things we have chosen to live with are not inert objects. We wrap our imaginations around them. We express ourselves through them. We make them into what we care about.

Sean Fitzpatrick played for the New Zealand All Blacks rugby team for 12 years. He was one of the greatest captains the game has known. He told me what place Love has in a game as hard-fought as rugby.

"To be in the All Blacks is about loving what you do. It's about caring for each other. The team is a family and you love your family. If you love your mate you're going to look after him and you're going to do anything for him.

"That's the beauty of playing in a team. You have 15 guys who all have one goal in mind rather than a set of individual goals. A collective goal. The aim is to be successful. The aim is to win and to do everything you can to make yourselves better players and better people. At the same time you want to help your mates be better players and better people, the same as you would for your brothers or your sisters."

Six truths about Love

The First one is a warning. **Human beings need Love. Without it they die.** Solitary people without Love are three to five times more likely to die early! Match this with plummeting birth rates in many Western countries and major increases in the number of people living alone, and you've got to say that the world needs a lot more loving in it.

Next comes a definition. **Love means more than liking a lot.** We are not talking affection plus. Love is about a profound sense of attachment. Want a really great metaphor? When researchers at Emory University in Atlanta track brain processes through scans, they can see different areas of the brain light up as they are engaged. How about that? We literally light up! If you want a definition of Love, that's not a bad one.

Third, **Love is about responding, about delicate, intuitive sensing.** Love is always two-way. When it is not, it cannot live up to the name Love. Some people will always be better at it than others, but we all have the capacity and need for Love.

Our Fourth truth concerns **who and what we love.** Everyone knows about the glories of romantic Love, but let's not forget the Love between couples who have been together for years, Love within families, the Love of close friends–very different relationships that join the experiences we love. For me, it's Bruce Springsteen concerts, Saturday nights, and a cold Becks beer. Whatever turns you on.

Fifth, **Love takes time.** The skill of responding to the emotional rhythms of Love takes an investment of years. Love has history. Love gives us meaning and makes us who we are.

Finally, and perhaps most profoundly, **Love cannot be commanded or demanded.** It can only be given. Like power, you get Love by giving it.

" I don't think there is anything higher than Love. I mean, I'm not sure what could possibly come after Love because Love is so expansive. I had such a difficult time coming up with a definition for Love in my book, but the way I define Love is the selfless promotion of the growth of the other.

So to me, if you selflessly promote the growth of your customers and your colleagues, that's true Love. I don't know what more you could do for someone. "

[Tim Sanders, Chief Solutions Officer, Yahoo!, and author of *Love Is the Killer App*]

" Whenever someone asks me to define Love, I usually think for a minute, then I spin around and pin the guy's arm behind his back. Now who's asking the questions? "

[Jack Handey, comic]

"I may not be a smart man, but I do know what Love is."
[Forrest Gump]

"Love: Two minds without a single thought."
[Philip Barry]

"Ah, good ol' trustworthy beer. My Love for you will never die."
[Homer Simpson]

"When Love and skill work together, expect a masterpiece."
[John Ruskin]

"Love doesn't make the world go 'round. Love is what makes the ride worthwhile."
[Franklin P. Jones]

"People think Love is an emotion. Love is good sense."
[Ken Kesey]

"I Love Mickey Mouse more than any woman I've ever known."
[Walt Disney]

"Love keeps the cold out better than a cloak."
[Henry Wadsworth Longfellow]

"Love does not consist of gazing at each other, but in looking outward together in the same direction."
[Antoine de Saint-Exupéry]

"Love is a canvas pattern furnished by Nature, and embroidered by imagination."
[Voltaire]

"Love is the only sane and satisfactory answer to the problem of human existence."
[Erich Fromm]

"I'm in favor of Love as long as it doesn't happen when the Simpsons are on TV."
[Anita–age 6]

Love is like oxygen

As I watched Saatchi & Saatchi show-reels of television
commercials in my first months on the job in 1997,
I became convinced that only an emotion like Love
could power the next evolution of branding. I could see
that Saatchi & Saatchi had made the first critical step in
creating emotional connections.

In the rational world of brand management, with its
drive to increase functional and performance benefits,
the ad agencies were called in at the tail end of the
marketing process to squirt on the emotional icing.
No wonder they got so little respect for doing it. We
needed to stand for more. Much more. What we needed
to stand for was Love.

When the Love Bug virus hit computers around the
world in 2000 I knew I was on the right track. Techno-
cool, hard-edged geeks did the unspeakable: clicked on
an unknown attachment. And all because someone said,
"I love you." We were onto a profound emotional need.

When I first suggested that Love was the way to transform business, grown CEOs blushed and slid down behind their annual accounts. But I kept at them.

I knew it was Love that was missing. I knew that Love was the only way to ante up the emotional temperature and create the new kinds of relationships brands needed.

I knew that Love was the only way businesses could respond to the rapid shift in control to consumers.

Once we got comfortable with saying the "L" word, we delved more deeply into understanding its breadth and relevance to business. We wondered about a way to rank brands or anything else according to the intensity of Love people felt for them. The really great things would be placed near the top with lesser ones towards the bottom.

Conventional wisdom says that brands are taking over people's lives. And that this is a bad thing. But maybe it works the other way. Maybe life is taking over brands.

What if we could use the same idea to account for people's passionate devotion to places, nations, and religions? To small local businesses as well as global brands, events as well as intimate experiences?

WHAT IF

• • •   forming long-term emotional relationships could be more than a catchphrase?

• • •   brands could grow and evolve with richer and deeper connections in the same way that people can in their lives?

• • •   the emotion that could make this transformation was Love?…

But Love built on what?

Chapter 5

GIMME SOME RESPECT

The Lovemarks of this new century will be the brands and businesses that create genuine emotional connections with the communities and networks they live in. This means getting up close and personal. And no one is going to let you get close enough to touch them unless they respect what you do and who you are.

Love needs Respect right from the start. Without it, Love will not last. It will fade like all passions and infatuations. Respect is what you need when you are in for the long haul.

Respect is one of the founding principles of Lovemarks.

"Respect is love in plain clothes."

[Frankie Byrne]

Management loves the idea of Respect. It sounds serious and objective, easily measured and managed. In fact, Respect has been prodded and squeezed so often over the last century that its real power has been undervalued. Respect is the foundation of successful business.

At Saatchi & Saatchi we decided one thing was mandatory from the get-go: No Respect, No Love.

But Respect needs to be reinvigorated. We need to understand what it demands. We need to expand our Respect metrics from financial and production performance to take on the deeper demands Respect makes of us. Respect looks to performance, reputation, and trust as its organizing principles. Within each of these principles I believe there is an inspiring code of conduct to lead you forward.

Perform, perform, perform

Respect grows out of performance. Performance at each and every interaction. Peak performance is the ultimate tablestake of all tablestakes.

Pursue innovation

Innovation is *kaizen*, continuous improvement, for consumers. Every business today is expected to innovate–and to innovate meaningfully while creating value.

Commit to total commitment

Going the full distance is the price of Respect. The new active consumer judges you at every encounter, every touchpoint, and will punish failure by not coming back.

Make it easy

The increasing complexity of many goods and services has raised the stakes. The equation is simple. If it's hard to use, it will die. Goodbye VCR. Hello DVD.

Don't hide

People can respect you only if they know who you are. Remember, in today's Internet environment there is nowhere you cannot be found. Don't even try.

Jealously guard your reputation

Built over a lifetime. Destroyed in an instant. Consumers today are ruthless if you let them down. So don't.

Get in the lead and stay there

To be out front can be lonely and uncomfortable, but remember, the lead husky gets the best view.

Tell the truth

Front up. Be open. Admit mistakes. Don't cover up, it will get you every time. Believe in yourself–at times like this it may be the only thing you have. And at times like this your reputation is your premium defense.

Nurture integrity

The corporate shake-ups of the last few years have put the spotlight back on integrity: the integrity of your people, your products, your services, your financial statements and, most importantly, your personal integrity.

Accept responsibility

Take on the biggest responsibility of all—to make the world a better place for everyone, creating self-esteem, wealth, prosperity, jobs, and choices. Quality is the measure by which you exceed expectations. Quality is all about standards. Keep it simple: set high standards and then exceed them. Meet, Beat, Repeat.

Never pull back on service

Service is where transactions are transformed into relationships. Where Respect meets Love. It is the first moment of truth.

Deliver great design

Attention Economy 101. Competition is hot and getting hotter. If you're not aesthetically stimulating and functionally effective you just merge into the crowd. You have to *be* different, not just *act* different.

Don't underestimate value

Not just real dollar value but the *perception* of value. Only when people perceive the value they are getting as higher than the cost will they respect the deal you offer. Sam Walton built Wal-Mart, the biggest retail empire in the world, by a relentless focus on best value.

Deserve trust

Consumers want to trust you. They want you to remain true to the ideals and aspirations you share with them. Practice what you preach. Never let them down.

Never, ever fail the reliability test

Expectations skyrocket: cars always start the first time, the coffee's always hot, the ATM is always open. Today reliability is the door charge for Respect before the show begins.

It's a tough list. Demanding and uncompromising. Don't even dream about Lovemark status unless you can tick off each and every item. The relationship between Respect and Love is deep, compelling, symbiotic. At the risk of repeating myself:

No Respect,
No Love,
No Respect,
No Love,
No Respect,
No Love,
Period.

1. Make innovation part of your everyday thinking. Insist on at least half an hour's blue-sky thinking by all your peoples every day.

2. Reward the tough questions. You want people to respect you and your business? First — show you respect their opinions.

3. Make quality control a fetish. There is no such thing as Perfect. The Japanese have taught us all through Kaizen that continuous improvement is money in the bank.

4. Bring design onto the front-burner. Great design is the gateway to great customer response.

5. Don't do secret stuff. Do a secrets audit. Examine each one and find out why you are keeping them — and at what potential risk.

Five things to do tomorrow

Chapter 6

LOVE IS IN THE AIR

Long before I joined Saatchi & Saatchi, I was aware that brands were entering an endgame. Being invited to be CEO of the most exciting advertising agency in the world certainly sharpened my focus. It was all very well knowing the problems with brands, but what was the solution?

How could we inspire brands to evolve to the next level? The usual stuff like organizational change, rejigging structure, and smarter logistics wasn't going to do it.

There had to be something new, something that would create

Loyalty Beyond Reason.

My thinking started to crystallize around a line Tide used back in the 1970s. "Tide for cleaning you can count on." I thought, "Something you could always count on. That would be hugely valuable. That *would* be Loyalty Beyond Reason."

And the first word that came to me was trust. Many of our clients responded to the idea of trust. The Internet had put trust firmly on the agenda. Trust felt like part of the vocabulary.

I was hot on the trail of something I thought of as Trustmarks when I met Alan Webber, Founding Editor of the business magazine *Fast Company*. We were at a top-to-top CEO forum at Cambridge University convened by P&G. Here's how Alan remembers it:

"What happened was, we began to talk to each other about what Kevin might have that could turn into something for *Fast Company*. What I do as an editor, basically, is listen to people talk. And frequently they turn a phrase or use a construction of language that just sounds like the name of an article waiting to be written. Maybe they know it and maybe they don't. Sometimes they know it but they haven't yet popped it up to the level of importance that it's worth. That's what happened in those round-table conversations at Cambridge.

"In my notebooks I just kept circling some of the language that Kevin was using. He was talking about the emotions of marketing and the need to migrate from a brand to the next levels of emotional commitment. That struck me as a very smart observation. We'd done a lot of stuff in the five or so years that *Fast Company* had existed about branding. Like Tom Peters on the brand called 'You' and other marketers who were trying to define what branding meant. Yet here was a guy who was saying branding is tablestakes! Old news. What you've got to do is go beyond the brand to the emotions that take you deeper into the relation-ship you have with your consumer or your potential audience. So I was following that up with him, and out of that came a conversation that stretched both of us."

[Alan Webber, Founding Editor, *Fast Company*]

Alan was right onto my ideas about a new state beyond brands. A few weeks later he set up an interview to shake out my thinking and we were off. The results were published as "Trust in the Future" in the September 2000 issue of *Fast Company*.

From the start we were talking *tough* Love. We knew that consumers were cynical, savvy, and selective. They didn't give a stuff about famous brands. They wanted more. I felt the same way. Big-time brand? Big deal!

You've got three seconds to impress me. Three seconds to connect with me, to make me fall in Love with your product.

Tough lines for a whole heap of big-name brands, but as the old saying goes, "If you keep doing what you're doing you just keep getting what you're getting."

Moving up the food chain from brands was the big goal, but we still didn't have the right word for it. We were talking Trustmarks, but did that name sing? We knew what a trademark was: a differentiator, a distinctive name or symbol that legally identified a company or its products. But what was a Trustmark?

I was already convinced that there was no way a Trustmark could be owned by a company. That was part of the problem with brands. It was why consumers were feeling alienated. No, if anyone was going to own Trustmarks it was going to be consumers!

But even trust wasn't going to be enough to make the big leap. I mean, just trusting someone isn't going to bind you for life. And nothing short of a lifelong relationship was the sort of commitment I was looking for.

The answer came towards the end of our discussion. Trustmarks weren't going to do it. Sure they were sensible, credible, even acceptable, but they lacked emotion and drive. A Trustmark might make things better, but it was never going to transform anything. Time to take a deep breath and leap to the next level. As I said to Alan in our *Fast Company* interview:

trust *in the future*

"Trustmarks come after brands; Lovemarks come after Trustmarks....Think about how you make the most money. You make it when loyal users, heavy users, use your product all the time. That's where the money is. So having a long-term Love affair is better than having a trusting relationship."

Could I get my brand to be Loved as well as trusted?

My ideas were based on work we had done comparing brands with what we now know were emerging as Lovemarks. The best brands were Trustmarks, we had decided, but the great ones were Lovemarks. We charted the differences.

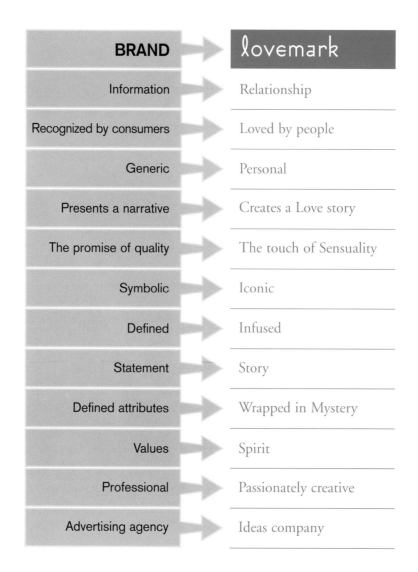

BRAND	lovemark
Information	Relationship
Recognized by consumers	Loved by people
Generic	Personal
Presents a narrative	Creates a Love story
The promise of quality	The touch of Sensuality
Symbolic	Iconic
Defined	Infused
Statement	Story
Defined attributes	Wrapped in Mystery
Values	Spirit
Professional	Passionately creative
Advertising agency	Ideas company

I said in the article:

> "I'm sure that you can charge a premium for brands that people love.
> And I'm also sure that you can only have one Lovemark in any category."

I was sure then, but now I see I was wrong. Now that we have moved more deeply into Lovemarks we can see that this was way too narrow. The sushi shop on the corner of your block can be a Lovemark to you. Lovemarks can be created by designers, producers, service people, cities, and nations.

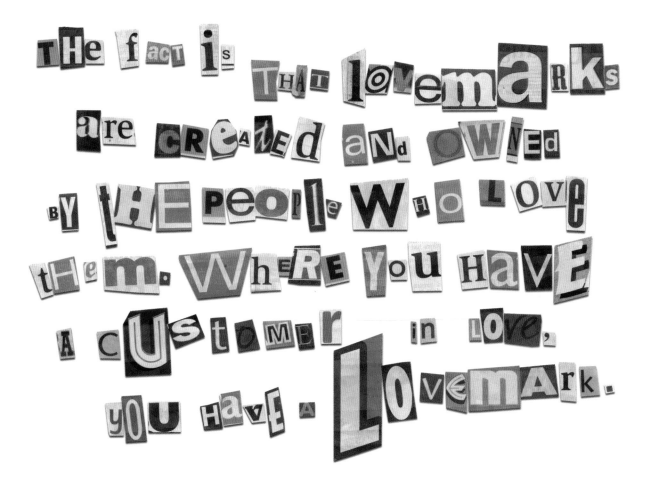

The fact is that lovemarks are created and owned by the people who love them. Where you have a customer in love, you have a Lovemark.

Can consumers make Lovemarks out of two products in the same category? As far as I'm concerned, they can do anything they damn well please!

"One of the things that we all learn in our business careers is that language matters. That has been a hallmark of *Fast Company*. If you describe something or name something accurately, that coinage becomes not just a marketable product, it fundamentally changes the conversation, and people begin to reframe the way they think and talk to each other. They begin to create categories in their own business experience they didn't even know existed.

"I definitely feel that's what our article with Kevin did. It opened up a whole new category where people could think about the way their companies perform. It's interesting that a recent Nobel prize for economics went to a couple of economists who were, once and for all, making it an official, acceptable fact that the most important part of economics is emotional. That emotion is one of the key elements of economic behavior.

"One of the points Kevin was making in our article—and obviously it has emerged even more strongly—is that the way you relate to the market is, in many respects, making manifest that which is fundamentally intangible. It's not about the cost per thousand, or the rate, or what you are charging for this product. It's the way it feels, the way it represents itself, and then the way it either does or doesn't live up to those representations."

[Alan Webber, Founding Editor, *Fast Company*]

Chapter 7

BEAUTIFUL
OBSESSION

Lovemarks made immediate sense. Every person we deal with is an emotional human being, and yet business had been treating them like numbers. Targets. Statistics.

Respect was something that Saatchi & Saatchi understood. Over the years we had put a lot of time into building our clients' products into some of the most highly respected brands in the world. Now it was time to focus on what made some brands stand out from the crowd. What made some brands Loved.

When it came to working out what gave Lovemarks their special emotional resonance, we came pretty quickly to:

Mystery
Sensuality
Intimacy

These didn't sound like traditional brand attributes. And they captured the new emotional connections we were seeking. As I have already mentioned, we were convinced from the start by a very important idea that became the heart of Lovemarks.

Lovemarks are not owned by the manufacturers, the producers, the businesses. They are owned by the people who love them.

From there it was easy to agree that you only get to be a Lovemark when the people who love you tell you so. But just sitting around waiting for consumers to tell you you're a Lovemark could mean a very long wait.

Love is about action. It's about creating a meaningful relationship. It's a constant process of keeping in touch, working with consumers, understanding them, spending time with them. And this is what insightful marketers, empathetic designers, and smart people on the checkout and production line do every day.

Now we were ready to create our principles.

BE PASSIONATE

Consumers can smell a fake a mile off. If you're not in Love with your own business, they won't be either.

INVOLVE CUSTOMERS

They need to be brought into advising on new product development and working up ideas for services. Involve them in everything, but there is no point in just reflecting back what they have already told you. Make your own commitment to change. Be creative.

CELEBRATE LOYALTY

"Will you still love me tomorrow?" Loyalty demands consistency. Change is fine, but both partners must be full participants.

FIND, TELL, & RETELL GREAT STORIES

Lovemarks are infused with powerful and evocative stories. At their best these grow into mythical tales. They recall the great adventures of the business, its products and their legendary consumers. Storytelling gives luster by opening up new meanings, connections, and feelings.

ACCEPT RESPONSIBILITY

Lovemarks are, by definition, top of their class for the people who love them. The passion for a Lovemark can be intense. At the far end of the scale people will lay down their lives for a Lovemark. In fact, nations may well be some of the most powerful Lovemarks of them all.

We were seeing Lovemarks as highly charged emotional relationships. Whenever we talked Lovemarks we found ourselves referring to people we knew or had heard of.

We asked ourselves:

How do families build up their vast reservoirs of Love? What Love inspires people to become extraordinary? When times are tough what kind of Love do people call on to see them through? What builds Loyalty that goes Beyond Reason?

WHAT MAKES A TRULY GREAT LOVE STAND OUT?

Lovemarks could not be constrained by the world defined by brands and marketing. Sure this world was important, but Lovemarks had to be open to more. Open to the local and to the global. To connect with people as well as services. Places as well as products. The objects people make themselves as well as what they buy.

Constantly testing our ideas against everything that people love, we agreed that Mystery, Sensuality, and Intimacy are made up of the following elements:

Mystery

Great stories
Past, present, and future
Taps into dreams
Myths and icons
Inspiration

Sensuality

Sound
Sight
Smell
Touch
Taste

Intimacy

Commitment
Empathy
Passion

This was what we needed to generate ideas and insights. We were determined that Lovemarks were going to be more than an idea that could transform brands and marketing. They had to be a new point of view. A way to change how companies see themselves and how they feel about consumers. And, as importantly, to change how consumers feel about business.

Lovemarks would become nothing less than the future beyond brands.

We created a test. We decided a brand might be a Lovemark if it matched up to these statements:

- Lovemarks connect companies, their people and their brands
- Lovemarks inspire Loyalty Beyond Reason
- Lovemarks are owned by the people who love them

This was exciting. If Lovemarks could step up to this level, they would become the ultimate premium-profit generators. Darwin would have got it right off. Fish to lizard. Monkey to man. Brand to Lovemark. An evolutionary stairway to heaven.

We also began to play with suggestions as to what brands might already fit into our Lovemark framework. After all, this was an idea that had emerged from what a select band of stellar performers were already doing brilliantly.

"If something gets to be a billion-dollar brand, there's more going on than just a rational attachment. My feeling is that all the billion-dollar brands occupy a very special place in the heart among some consumers. That would make them Lovemarks."

[Jim Stengel, Global Marketing Officer, Procter & Gamble]

A few jumped out. Not just major global brands, but brands with a strong emotional connection with consumers. Brands with a passionate group of people who loved them. Brands inspiring Loyalty Beyond Reason.

Harley-Davidson was one. We had all heard about how they had risen from the dead, creating devoted customers and delivering outstanding financial performance. Excited, we ran through our Lovemarks characteristics. Harley's score was off the charts–Mystery, Sensuality, and Intimacy to burn.

The iPod? Fantastic. Coca-Cola? Another hit. Virgin Atlantic? Just ask Ben, my eldest son!

We then got a list of top global brands and thought about which ones seemed to us to be Lovemarks. We asked people around Saatchi & Saatchi what they thought, and instantly we found ourselves caught up in intense conversations.

From these discussions we gathered together the most popular suggestions to see how Lovemarks stacked up as a practical idea.

Even now, looking back, most of the brands we included on that early list still look pretty good. In terms of our key elements–Mystery, Sensuality, and Intimacy– our top 25 gave us a lot to think about. Some made it in all three areas, some didn't.

Amazon, Apple, The Body Shop, CNN, Coca-Cola, Disney, Dyson, eBay, Google, Harley-Davidson, Italy, LEGO, Levi's, McDonald's, Manchester United, Nelson Mandela, Nike, Nintendo, Nokia, Pampers, Red Cross, Swatch, Toyota, Vespa, Virgin.

One thing that our Lovemark list did confirm: Lovemarks are personal. And they can be anything–a person, a country, a car, an organization. Lovemarks are the charismatic brands that people love and fiercely protect. For keeps. You know them instantly.

"Great brands have always been Lovemarks. What Lovemarks have done is give a structure in which to think about that. But I think as long as there have been brands with emotional attachments and connections and loyalty, there have been Lovemarks.

"One way to think about what a Lovemark might be is to consider how a consumer would feel if you took the brand away. What would the person's reaction be? In our own business I know if you take away the Pampers that worked exceptionally well for her child, the mother will have a very strong reaction! If you take away a CoverGirl lip shade that looks just great with her coloring from a teenager, she will be angry. If you take away Tide with bleach, if you take away Ariel from loyal users, they will be angry. So these are measures of an emotional connection and an attachment to the brand that goes beyond reason."

[Jim Stengel, Global Marketing Officer, Procter & Gamble]

The next task was to look carefully at

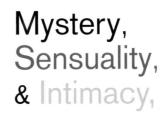

Mystery,
Sensuality,
& Intimacy,

and develop our ideas.

We were in for a few surprises.

1. Make at least 3 consumer connections a week
The only way to find out what consumers are thinking is to talk to them and listen to what they have to say. They won't say these things to you on visit one — so do repeats.

2. Look at the list of Lovemark companies in this chapter. Take two you like and work out how they use Mystery, Sensuality and Intimacy to grow their businesses.

3. Find three businesses you admire in your own category and study how they form emotional relationships with their consumers.

4. Reward Loyalty. Make some small, spontaneous gestures to folk who have stood by you. Do it tomorrow.

5. Find someone who is Loyal Beyond Reason — to anything; a car, a hobby, a friend. Find out what makes it work and apply it to your business.

Five things
to do tomorrow

Chapter 8

ALL I HAVE
TO DO IS DREAM

"I'll never understand you as long as I live!"

Of everything people say in a long-term loving relationship, that's the killer. The one that sums it up.

Great relationships thrive on learning, anticipation, and surprise. When you know everything there is to know, there is nothing left to discover. No more wonder, no more opportunities.

No more relationships.

How many relationships come adrift because the spark goes out? And how often do experts and counselors prescribe more Mystery and surprise to re-ignite what has gone flat?

After giving a sermon on the Creation, a minister was surprised to hear an elderly parishioner tell him that she believed that the world rested on the back of a turtle. Trying to let her down lightly, he asked what she thought held the turtle up. Rather puzzled, she replied "Another turtle, of course." The minister pushed harder. "Okay then, so what holds that turtle up?" "Another turtle," she said. "And don't get your hopes up, young man. It's turtles, all the way down."

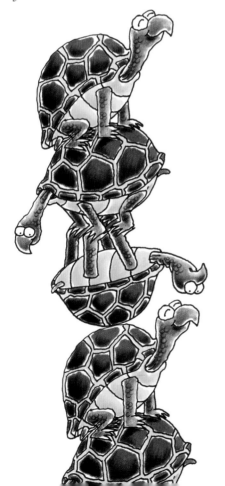

When we were working through the essentials of a Lovemark, Mystery was always at the top of the list. This may seem counterintuitive. Business people often feel that the more numbers they can throw at a brand, the more credibility sticks. This may get them to tag along with the march of scientific progress, but always at the expense of Mystery.

Fortunately, Mystery is a paradox. The more you strip away, the more Mysteries you find. Ask neurologists, cosmologists, biologists, and all the other "-ists." They will all tell you the same process goes on to infinity—just like the turtles.

As a child, I found highly detailed explanations numbing. And all of us at one time or another have felt the sobering pseudo-reality of numbers dump on what seemed to be an exciting idea.

Remember the disappointment when you finally persuaded a friend to show you how a magic trick was done? One minute you believed you had seen the impossible. The next, you were irritated to find out how easily you had been fooled. What a bum trade. Magic for trickery.

Most businesses are obsessed with downplaying Mystery. They are determined to frame the world so it fits their own systems and processes.

No wonder they find it tough to communicate with anyone, including their own people. They pump out specifications, details, and diagrams. Define this benefit, delineate that target. Write plans and strategies backed up with statistics. Gives me a headache just thinking about it. And it's not going to work. It is not going to work in the airline business, the food business, the cleaning business, or any other business. How can it? Every major industry player now has exactly the same data, the same research suppliers, the same techniques, the same processes, and, in many cases, the same people, who've just changed companies but stayed in the industry. As Pete Seeger famously sang: "There's a green one and a pink one and a blue one and a yellow one, and they're all made out of ticky-tacky and they all look just the same."

As long as people have aspirations and goals and dreams, they will always crave Mystery. Whoever heard of anyone craving…statistics?

The great thing about Mystery is that it is beyond rationality, beyond calculation.

But Mystery is under pressure everywhere. From the bureaucrats, the incrementalists, the traditionalists, the we've-never-had-it-so-good brigade, the don't-rock-the-boat crew, and of course, the cult of the Village Green Preservation Society! And it is eroding before our eyes. Taking action on Mystery sounds paradoxical, but that is exactly what we must do. Creating Mystery is an art.

"We named our company Putumayo after an area of southern Colombia which is itself named after a river that starts in the foothills of the Andes. In the Putumayo region there is a small village which was one of my favorite places to go. It was one of those really magical areas. The first time I happened to show up was during one of their carnival celebrations. I remember waking up the next morning, sitting by the side of a little stream that led into the Putumayo River. The Andes were in the background, birds were flying around, and the Indians were going and coming from their fields. It felt like all was right with the world.

"It would be nice for people caught up in the hustle and craziness of big cities like New York to be able to travel all the time to places like Putumayo, but they can't always do that.

"So in a way what we've done with Putumayo World Music has always been kind of an attempt to try and help people travel the world. To let them explore other cultures and have a taste of the mystery and appeal of World Music. To let them discover how by being melodic and upbeat it helps people rise above their daily problems. It makes you feel good and becomes a positive element that has been created in another culture. I believe it is the positive side of the human spirit, and that music is one of the positive elements that human beings create.

"I also believe that, ultimately, the same thing drives people everywhere. That is, to try and find ways to make their lives happier and more meaningful. Unfortunately, there aren't that many things that do it. But music is one of those things."

[Dan Storper, Putumayo World Music]

If you believe in Mystery, clap your hands.

Peter Pan got it right. When Tinkerbell was clocking out because no one believed in her anymore, he asked the children of the world to revive her by clapping. Loudly. It worked. That is what Mystery needs, a surge of faith in its power.

The power of Mystery. You know it when you feel it. Marilyn Monroe had Mystery. Still does. Russell Crowe has got it—as a dangerous skinhead in *Romper Stomper* to Maximus to a reclusive mathematical genius.

The cloak of Mystery forces us to find our own meanings, our own sense of what is important in our lives. And it often does it through a revelation, a thunderbolt. What the French call a *coup de foudre*. Everything changes. This is what made *The Lord of the Rings*, Chanel No. 5, and Red Bull into Lovemarks for their devotees.

Mystery opens up emotion. Mystery adds to the complexity of relationships and experiences. It lies in the stories, metaphors, and iconic characters that give a relationship its texture. Mystery is a key part of creating Loyalty Beyond Reason.

A visionary at *Visionaire*

Cecilia Dean understands the elusive charm of Mystery. With her partners Stephen Gan and James Kaliardos, she co-founded in 1991 the extraordinary publication *Visionaire*. Issuing out of New York three or four times a year, *Visionaire* is a testament to the power of Mystery.

It has an exclusive reputation. Complete editorial integrity. A hip address in SoHo. World-beating image-makers. An unlikely marriage of fashion and contemporary art. All inspired by a new theme for each issue: flipbooks, Louis Vuitton satchels, injection-molded plastic cases, vintage novels. Each issue reinvents the concept of *Visionaire* and plays with the infinite possibilities of form and content.

I see copies of *Visionaire* on the tables of Saatchi & Saatchi creatives throughout the world. Why? Because it gives them a heady mix of sophistication and Mystery, inspiring ideas wrapped into a surprising and sensual object.

"I think mystery is really, really important. It's why we invite very few people into the back offices of *Visionaire*! One of the biggest downfalls of Hollywood is that celebrities no longer have any mystery. Having all your dirty laundry in every tabloid is not what I call deeply mysterious. Unfortunately most of these celebrities are just like you and me. Who wants always to be reminded of that?

"Being mysterious is becoming more difficult. We are dealing with a public that is so educated. I remember my 15-year-old sister understanding the difference between editorial and advertising! She knew that editorial was driven by advertising. I said, 'How do you know that? I didn't tell you that.' And she said, 'They know. People know.' Because they *do* know, you have to think of new ways to create mystery. Of course, in the creative field you can't help but be slightly mysterious. The whole process is mysterious. We have to deal with it every day–and *I* can't even explain it.

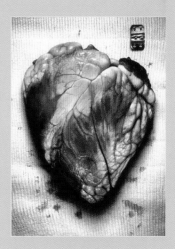

"With the *Love* issue we wanted to do something that really came from the heart. We'd done erotica and we'd done desire, so for us it was important to do something with a very innocent, pure type of Love.

"Stephen said, 'Let's find thousands of romance novels.' And that really started driving the issue. There was this idea that each book was going to be different and that they all had to be hardcover novels, hopefully with a Love story. Practically every novel has Love in it anyway, so that was not too hard. And then on top of all these different novels, we were getting highly personal work from these great photographers, so it started coming together like that.

"Our question to our contributors was: What is Love? What does it look like? What do you do out of Love and for Love?"

[Cecilia Dean, Creative Director, *Visionaire*]

Mystery's high five

Great stories; combining the past, present, and future; tapping into dreams; great myths and icons; and instilling inspiration.

1. Tell your stories

Stories feed Lovemarks. They are how we explain the world to ourselves and give value to the things we love. We all know how a great story at the right moment can change our minds or release that vital "Oh-now-I-get-it."

The Māori people of New Zealand talk about surrounding their great treasures with "interesting talk." This, they believe, increases the *mana* (standing) of the object. I believe this too. I have seen "interesting talk" work its magic time after time.

Just before Buck Shelford, an inspirational leader and captain of New Zealand's All Blacks rugby team, led his players onto the field to defend the nation's pride, his final words drew on his own Māori heritage. *Kia Kaha.* Be Strong. For every All Black, no opposition is as intimidating as their own legacy.

The world of information is a tough place to stimulate any change of emotion or action. Lovemarks use stories to show why information matters.

That word "content" depresses me. No point of view. No energy. A generic label for generic stuff. Shovel-ware. It's for sworn-in members of the commodification mafia.

Stories have huge value in business because they look in the right direction. At people. You cannot tell a story without characters and emotion and sensory detail. Even the dumbest road-crossing-chicken jokes have it. And they capture us faster than the most elaborately produced annual report.

Q: Why did the chicken cross the road? ——————— A: To prove to the possum it could actually be done!

A picture may be worth a thousand words, but terrific stories are right up there with them.

So it is no surprise that 30-second television commercials can create powerful emotional connections like nothing else. They are the most compelling selling tool ever invented.

People who say that television ads are a thing of the past just don't get it. First, they thought that 500 channels would kill off TV ads. But no, media buyers just picked the channels people watched. Same story with TiVo and any other filtering devices anyone wants to put up.

What people hate are boring 30-second commercials. Great 30-second commercials, they love. That's why there are whole TV shows that play nothing but commercials. And why do people love them? Because they tell stories. And people love being told a story.

Annette Simmons is an expert in storytelling. She touches the central point precisely: "When you tell a story that touches me, you give me the gift of human attention–the kind that connects me to you, that touches my heart and makes me feel more alive."

Advertising is part of pop culture, like music, TV, movies, celebrity gossip. The stuff of the context of our lives. We talk about great ads in bars, on buses, at work, with our families, around the watercooler. We rarely debate statistics there.

A great story can never be told too often.

Just look at the ones that endure to become myths and legends. Why? Because there is always someone new ready to listen for the first time.

Lexus has always valued stories. They may not use them in advertising, but they permeate the Lexus culture, and especially the dealerships. And often it is the dealers who turn out to be the heroes of great stories.

My favorite Lexus story? Imagine you're in your Lexus driving to the hospital with your pregnant wife. You know you are not going to make it and just then your local Lexus dealership comes into view. That is exactly what happened to Mark and his wife. They pulled in and with the help of the Lexus people delivered the baby. But the support didn't stop there. They loaned him another car, cleaned up his, and generally played proud relatives. What could Mark and his wife do in return? They named their daughter Isabella Alexus.

The James Bond franchise, launched in 1962 with *Dr. No*, has also got a lot to tell us about long-term success in the multi-billion dollar entertainment industry. The question has got to be: Why is this Englishman who is constantly pitted against global crime czars still with us? Many others have tried to topple him, but even the Terminator was no match for the spiffy British spy.

The reason is simple. The legendary movie magnate Samuel Goldwyn nailed it:

James Bond movies tell a simple story, tell it well, and tell it every time. Lovemarks adapt to new generations of consumers while being very clear about their story.

Then there is the Spanish company, Camper. They start with the story of Majorca, the island in Spain where Camper was born in 1976, but they also reach backwards to absorb the craft and skill of generations of shoemakers long before Camper itself was established. By attaching themselves in this way to tradition, the company very consciously created an overall Camper style and philosophy of life, and a story of origin and tradition.

"if you can't write your movie idea on the back of a business card, you ain't got a movie."

Paradoxically, this solid foundation in the past has pushed them forward to make some of the hippest shoes around. Shoes where some styles have a different-sized right foot and left foot. Shoes that may have messages and poems inscribed into their soles. Shoes with stories on the labels.

Lovemarks know how to mine and treasure their stories. They know that stories are told by people, by individuals. You can't work them up on a whiteboard in a meeting room and still expect them to connect.

Where do the real stories come from? From people. From the people who love what you do, and from the people who may not love you but care enough to respond.

Great brands have always been surrounded by great stories. Brands aspiring to be Lovemarks must develop intuitive listening skills and ways to harvest stories of their consumer experiences.

2. Use your past, present, and future

Lovemarks are like the best families–they combine learning from the past with the dynamics of the present to create great futures. Acknowledging how the past, present, and future are entwined was one of the guiding principles of Walt Disney as he built the Disney Corporation out of a short cartoon about a mouse.

"To all that come to this happy place: Welcome. Disneyland is your land. Here age relives fond memories of the past, and here youth may savor the challenge and promise of the future. Disneyland is dedicated to the ideals, the dreams, and the hard facts that have created America…with hope that it will be a source of joy and inspiration to the world."

[Memorial to Walt Disney at the gates of Disneyland in Anaheim, California]

When you experience something you feel might be a Lovemark, check out how it acknowledges the past as it heads to the future. No connections–no Lovemark.

I'm not talking about cheap nostalgia, but the unshakeable conviction that the past shapes the present.

Watching businesses shed their history like so much unwanted skin makes me sad. What a waste.

Why do great generals study battles from earlier times? Not to work out troop deployment, that's for sure. They are looking for evidence of how people react to extreme situations. How they react emotionally. And how they can use these insights.

It is said that there are 364 days to practice… and one St. Patrick's Day. This is the Irish spirit that has inspired Guinness to become a world-famous Lovemark. Fueled by the renaissance of Irish culture since the 1980s, the Guinness brand has wasted no time in staking its claim to the Irish past, present, and future everywhere. Especially in Jim O'Mahony and Stan O'Keefe's pub, Warners, in Cathedral Square in Christchurch, New Zealand.

The Guinness Storehouse visitor center in Dublin transformed the old St. James' Gate Brewery into the "Home, Heart, and Soul of Guinness Beer." Set to become a major tourist attraction, the Storehouse deeply connects the Guinness brand with Irish national history.

Then, when you add a powerfully emotional link to the 3,000 or so Irish pubs around the world selling the Irish dream, you have what comes close to a religious movement.

The genius of the Guinness brand is that it doesn't only connect with people in places to which the Irish have emigrated. Guinness beer was first exported to Africa in 1827, and from this foundation an extraordinary tradition has grown up. The Guinness brand in Africa speaks of the future as well as the past. The luck of the Irish indeed.

Some companies make the most of their heritage and still can draw it brilliantly into the present. Take the German automobile

Audi. The classic logo embodies the fact that its past, present, and future are inextricably entwined. The four silver rings represent the four companies (Wanderer, DKW, Horch, and Audi) that came together in 1932 to form the Auto Union that became Audi. How then could they resist becoming the official car of the *Lord of the Rings* trilogy?

Lovemarks know that their emotional legacy can inspire passion for current projects and inspire Loyalty Beyond Reason. Look at Cheerios, a great American Lovemark. Over the years, our client General Mills has understood that, to millions of American families, Cheerios is more than just a breakfast cereal. For instance, it can be a target. Some little boys are taught to aim with the help of a Cheerio ring in the bottom of the potty!

The creation of a Lovemark is cumulative. If you don't understand what you mean to the grandparents, it's tough to understand what the next generation needs. This is why a Lovemark never freezes in place. If you can't respond, there is no way you can be a Lovemark.

If you want to see the past, present, and future working brilliantly together, look to sport.

When I was working on the book *Peak Performance* with my colleagues Clive Gilson, Mike Pratt, and Ed Weymes from Waikato Management School, we found that successful teams always lionize their past. The New Zealand All Blacks are my own favorite team,

my personal Lovemark. They are one of the most successful teams in the history of sport. The All Blacks have a saying that sums it up: "Preserving your body never enters your mind. Preserving your history never leaves it."

3. Tap into dreams

Dreams create action and action inspires dreams. Now that's what I call a virtuous cycle! It all comes down to this. If we know what consumers dream, it can only be because we are trusted and loved.

Brands wasted years fixating on information, boring people rigid with stuff they didn't want to know.

Lovemarks know that the people who love them are passionate, emotional, and often irrational human beings. What they are not are statistics or bullet points in the findings of some nerdy focus group.

It's all about listening. Not just keeping your mouth closed between each of your brilliant statements, but really listening.

Tapping into dreams is a powerful way of showing people that we understand their desires and can transform them into delight. The relationship between brands and consumers has been irrevocably changed. The change is a big one. And so are the rewards.

Maurice Lévy, Chairman of Publicis Groupe, sums it up:

"The idea of moving from a brand to a Lovemark means, for me, changing the relationship between the consumer and the brand. This change is from a rational decision to buy a brand to an irrational, passionate decision to be loyal to that brand. And you will find that, as the brand becomes a Lovemark, it will be forgiven for its mistakes. Lack of innovation, perhaps not always the best timing or the best price. In a Lovemark the bond between the brand and the consumer is very strong. It has moved from a rational 'I'm buying this because it has me getting this or that' to 'I'm buying this because I really love it.' It is adding to something that we call in France *les gratifications psychologiques*. It's giving you something that we call *les suppléments d'âme*–supplementing the soul. Now you can build loyalty with the consumer, which goes far beyond what you can get by being a brand, or a mega-brand. It is a step which is fantastic to take."

And then there are the dreams that inspire businesses. The founding vision of Microsoft was a great one:

A computer on every desk and in every home.

Of course, around the late 1990s, their dream had been pretty well realized, so they began looking around for something fresh and new. The proles replaced the visionary. They decided on:

Empower people through great software–any time, any place, and on any device.

Gee, that's catchy! Back to the drawing board, guys. But how about this for an emotional and realizable dream?

"I believe this nation should commit itself to achieving the goal, before this decade is out, of landing a man on the Moon and returning him safely to the Earth."

[President John F. Kennedy, speech to U.S. Congress, May 25, 1961]

Neil Armstrong, Apollo 11, July 20, 1969: Mission accomplished.

One of the least understood business secrets of our time has to be Uncle Walt's:

"If you can dream it, you can do it."

The classic dream-merchants are Harley-Davidson. They revived their fortunes on the brilliant insight that the middle-aged still want to rock and roll.

They dream that one day they too will "put the map in the trash and ride."

No matter that you are riding to the rules of the road on Interstate highways, the Harley dream is as real as the roar. Freedom and the spirit of adventure rule.

Anita Roddick understood the power of dreams. It was her dreams that powered the passions of The Body Shop. From one tiny outlet in Brighton, England in 1976, The Body Shop has grown to more than 1,900 stores in almost 50 countries.

Anita Roddick's personal philosophy started a business empire fixed on corporate social responsibility. The Body Shop taps into the dreams of their consumers for a better world. The dream of mysterious and exotic ingredients—jojoba oil, bergamot, and calendula. And the Roddick dreams survived even after she stepped down as CEO. As one of The Body Shop ads so astutely stated:

"If you think you're too small to have an impact, try going to bed with a mosquito."

4. Nurture your myths and icons

Nothing cuts through everyday clutter better than myths and icons. Why? Because they are memorable and memory is the wellspring of the heart. Many great Lovemarks are also great icons.

The Sydney Opera House
Designed by the great Dane, Jørn Utzon, its swooping sails define Australian confidence and Sydney's emotional connection with the ocean. The inspiration came out of dividing a small wooden sphere like an orange. The original model is in the collection of the Museum of Modern Art (another icon) in New York.

Nike's Swoosh
A big tick for one of the most stunning branding campaigns of the 20th century. Nike's Swoosh Design trademark was designed by Carolyn Davidson in response to Philip Knight's brief that it suggest "movement." Sure moved a lot of sports gear and changed the face of logo design. Across the Internet, rogue websites plot the "Swooshification" of the world.

In times of crisis and danger the cross and crescent icons of the **International Red Cross** and **Red Crescent** Movement seize attention and emotion. They are symbols of real sanctuary and real aid. Founded in 1863, the Movement has made its icons live in the simplest possible way.

The International Red Cross and Red Crescent keep the promise they have made to alleviate human suffering wherever it may be found. The cross and the crescent give shape to that inspiring goal.

Hello Kitty
Born out of the Lovemarks idea that "a small gift can bring a big smile to a child," the famous Japanese cat with no mouth is justly loved by children–and teens–across the world.

Nelson Mandela
A man who has become a metaphor for doing what's right, and holding to your principles.

Starbucks
The medallion logo that signals the smell of fresh coffee around the world. How cool of this Seattle-based business to name themselves after a mythic character from the classic novel *Moby Dick*.

Smiley face
I often use this iconic image. From short-hand squiggles on the bottom of notes to the sunny yellow badge, the smiley face is a simple ray of sunshine.

Creating iconic characters for M&M's was a great idea. It propelled them past the founders Mr. Mars and Mr. Murrie to icon heaven. And when the colors Red and Yellow appointed themselves Spokescandies for the new millennium, the Love quotient went through the roof.

M&M's work as icons not only because of their compelling graphic character, but also because of their feisty attitude and style. Their humor and irreverence. The candies with the endearing self-centeredness. Big kids.

Lovemark relationships are demanding ones. It's not enough to get it, and then forget it. Icons need Love too. Familiarity can easily breed indifference. Or worse.

Like Lovemarks, icons too must respond to the hopes, fears, and needs of new generations.

The power of many icons comes from the touch of the person who created them. I have huge admiration for professional designers, but sometimes the professional process can blunt passion. A great icon is direct. It is a response to a need rather than a step in corporate development.

My pick for a future global Lovemark? Toyota's marvellous car for the 21st century, the Prius.

5. Build on inspiration

Inspiration: "a sudden brilliant or timely idea." That's a pretty good definition. Inspiration has the power to transform lives. It can help navigate through these crazy, wonderful, upside-down times.

I believe the most important thing any adult can do for a child, any leader can do for his or her people, any product can do for its owner, any event can do for its audience, is to inspire them.

Only inspirational brands can be Lovemarks. We found this out with some of the greatest sports teams in the world when I was researching the book *Peak Performance* with my colleagues.

Our question was, "How do elite organizations sustain Peak Performance?" We might also have asked, "And why are these organizations so often Lovemarks?"

Do you want to see Love in action? Go to a local game and watch the faces of the fans when the home team scores. Just think about it: what are the most watched television programs around the globe?

What an incredible experience to have secured the 2004 Olympic Games campaign for Saatchi & Saatchi. Nothing is Impossible? Believe it.

The Olympic Games have inspired generations of people throughout the world since the first modern Games in 1896. While they are now a marketing behemoth, they hold tightly to the inspiration that sets them apart from other events. The Olympic Spirit is characterized as Joy in Effort, Friendship and Fair Play, Dreams and Inspiration, and Hope.

With sensational icons like the rings, the torch, the flame, and the medals as well as the sensual excitement of the opening events and competitions, the Intimacy of personal achievement, and the passion of thousands of athletes competing–the Olympics is a textbook Lovemark. Any business that aspires to become a Lovemark should have at least one day-long workshop a year developing insights from this mighty sporting event.

Our research into teams that people are passionate about–the Australian cricket team, FC Bayern Munich, the New York Yankees–revealed the same inspirational spirit that typifies great Lovemarks.

As we wrote in *Peak Performance*: "They experience passion, elation, and heartache, and they secure meaning and purpose from their commitment to their chosen team and sports code."

You don't find inspiration only in sport. The French design giant Philippe Starck is innovative, smart, and poetic. I love that he made the Juicy Salif lemon squeezer for Alessi just because it looked so great. Even if this rocket-shaped marvel didn't put the squeeze on lemons, it would still be a fabulous thing to own. It's a design classic and bestseller. Starck has inspired millions of people who thought good-looking objects were only for the rich and to demand more of design for the stuff we use every day. As he said himself:

"The reign of the poetical has started."

I recently commissioned the New York artist Sean Landers to make a large painting he called "Becoming Great."

"When I was a teacher I would encourage my students to make things, almost on a whim, even if they didn't understand it. My reasoning was that while for a short time it would be a mystery to them, over the longer term, looking backwards, they would see a pattern that would start to make sense. There is an element of mystery involved in art.

"What makes artwork great is always between the idea and what actually goes through your arm and out to the canvas. It's always such a surprise, the result so different from what you're expecting.

"Over the years, I have learned to put myself in a position where accidents can happen and where I can take advantage of small mysteries. This is a strange process of discovery. I know that my initial idea is merely a point of departure, never the end.

"'Becoming Great' ended up as an image of thought. That's the way it looks to me. The way thoughts can be just flashes of things that hit you. Then at other points things that flow, one drifting into another. When I first began it, I never thought of it as kind of like a graphic image of thought. That just happened. So as it evolved there were all these discoveries. Things that came out of the unknown. Mysteries."

[Sean Landers, artist]

M AL...

HOPE SOME ...ONG

...T HIM THERE IS. LIKE

MINE, NOT IN THIS

E TYPE OF THING

IM LAST NIGHT.

ME. IN SHORT

1. Ask everyone you work with for a story that reflects what makes your brand special to them. The more diverse the stories, the richer the brand.

2. Call for all those questions about your brand that people "always wanted to know but were afraid to ask". (Thanks Woody Allen!) Make them your agenda for the next four weeks.

3. How would you tell consumers how much you personally love your brand? If you think they wouldn't care, re-think how you are talking with them.

4. Ask three friends — people not in the same business — for a story about one of your brands. If they haven't got ones, you have work to do.

5. Make a list of stories about your competitors that you wish were about your brand. Get out there and capture them for yourself.

Five things
to do tomorrow

Chapter 9

THE HUMAN TOUCH

My interest in Sensuality sprang out of a frustration with Tide. When I was with Procter & Gamble, I was convinced that it had a magnificent visual identity, the yellow-and-orange bull's-eye. But back then we only sold Tide on performance. The Tide bull's-eye was firmly in the background. And then I saw Neil Young in a recording studio wearing a sleeveless T-shirt with the Tide logo, and it just screamed possibilities.

I thought, "Hey that's not right. The Coca-Cola logo is every-where, and Tide's is nowhere to be seen."

Didn't make sense. Coca-Cola slakes thirst. Tide cleans dirt. And there's dirt everywhere there is thirst. Tide should be at the point of dirt. That means everywhere.

So we started investigating the senses, and found every one of them to be provocative, immediate, and full of praise. That was the sort of closeness I was after. Marie McNeely and her team then took Tide to the streets—and to record market shares.

In my apartment, the laundry is next to the bath-room. The day I moved in we did some cleaning. Tide. Downy. Bounce. Wow! When I walked into my bathroom, it smelled so fresh and so clean. Uplifting.

When it comes to the senses, there is one day I will never forget. My first visit to the Middle East in 1972. Beirut. The dazzling light and incredible textures, the chaos of traffic and people, the brilliant colors and the dark, ripe smells of a street market culture. You could taste the air.

After a couple of days there I was exhausted by the strange richness of it all. As someone who championed change, I still found myself overwhelmed. Like so many before me, I was experiencing culture shock. The cure? Take time out. Let your senses recover. Calm down. Assimilate. And then get back into it! Later, when I found out that, in English, the word for the "senses" comes from the Latin *sentire*, "to feel," it made perfect sense!

The senses are the fast track to human emotions.

Direct, provocative, immediate. Tough to fool. Even tougher to override. The senses speak to the mind in the language of emotions, not words. Emotions alert us to how important the findings of our senses are, not only to our well-being, but indeed to our very survival.

All of our knowledge comes to us through the senses, but they are far more than sophisticated gatherers of information. The senses interpret and prioritize. When we feel emotionally connected, we say, "That makes sense."

Lovemarks are created by emotional connections with consumers in ways that go beyond rational arguments and benefits. We need to learn the language of the senses to make this happen. But this is tougher than simply doing more–adding fragrance, taste, texture. Pumping up the volume.

In the sensual world, faster, brighter, louder hit the wall real quick. People turn off and you lose them. Lovemarks need Sensuality, but they need it with a human touch.

Why do sensualists get such a bad rap?

We should be combing the world for them.

The race to embrace the senses

Over the last 20 years, I have watched science and technology accelerate their mastery of the senses. High-tech instruments designed to measure minute effects. Hundreds of publications, patents, and trademarks.

What is driving this frenzy of activity? The understanding of how important the senses are to human decision-making and to persuasion. The misunderstanding of how this relationship works. But the approaches to date have been too narrow, too analytical, too rational, and too damn metric.

Lovemarks are the missing link.

There have been huge investments into sensual innovation over the last few decades. The Colonel's secret recipe, the shape of the Coca-Cola bottle, the scent of a thousand perfumes, home sound-systems to die for, fabrics that mimic every possible natural surface. If you can sense it, they are getting close to being able to make it.

The Economist tells us that the flavor and fragrance industries have global sales accounting for more than a third of the $35-billion-a-year food ingredients market. And this is just the start. The promise of biotechnology is virtually untapped.

It's a huge market, but still seriously lacking in two areas. Imagination and ideas. When I look at what is happening in the flavor, food, and fragrance industries around the world, I find them trapped in a race down the road to commodification. They are obsessed by all the stuff that should be treated as tablestakes: consistency, ease of production, efficiency. They push deeply into ingredients, shapes, and surfaces, but always to control their power, not unleash them.

Touch.
The limestone in my apartment.

Sight.
The white B&O stereo I had finished in New White. White.

Sound.
My iPod. 4,475 tracks on it so far!

Taste.
HP Sauce, bought from Myers of Keswick in the meat-packing district. My Lancaster roo...

Smell.
Tide. Downy. Bounce. The fragrance of summer.

These industries now need to connect with what people feel and want, not simply with what can be delivered. The only breakthroughs will only come with and/and. Taste *and* texture. Sight *and* sound. Taste *and* touch. Smell *and* taste.

Our senses work together, and when they are stimulated at the same time, the results are unforgettable. Ask anyone who has tried the dreaded Asian fruit, durian. Looks like an aggressive mango. Smells like a sewer.

For those who can get past the smell, the taste is supposed to be out of this world. But who can get close enough to prove it?

And it is where the senses work together that you find that indefinable sixth sense we call intuition. Impossible to measure, it gets discounted from every business equation. But when your focus is connecting with consumers, intuition matters.

Making sense of the senses

Sight, hearing, smell, touch, taste. We're all gifted with a wide array of senses. Conventionally, we have categorized them into the Big Five.

But don't forget our other vital senses, constantly monitoring our body: Are we warm or cold? Upright…or not? Getting enough oxygen? Putting one foot in front of the other? Are we walking?

The human senses are extraordinarily refined. Apparently we notice if synchronization of the senses is off by more than 50 microseconds!

It seems strange that as our lives and experiences have become more complex, we have tended to downplay our senses rather than pay more attention to their guidance. Yet it is still our senses that kick us into action. The smell of smoke puts us on full alert. Fight or flight? And the senses can also calm and soothe us. Stroking the smooth skin of a baby. Breathing in a salt-flavored breeze.

The range of our senses is extraordinary. Thank evolution once again. The world constantly changes. Who won the evolution game? Hands up. Answer: the ones who responded fastest to the widest range of stimulation and information. And they won hands down.

The senses alert us, enflame us, warn us as well as fill our hearts with joy. They have protected and enriched us throughout our evolutionary story.

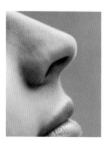

Without Sensuality our existence would become unbearably bland and ultimately, impossible.

Crayola, it turns out, are sensualists after my own heart. Their passion is to combine color, smell, and the feel of the crayons on the page into an unforgettable sensual experience. Their success has been so great that the Smithsonian Institution in Washington, D.C. told their story.

The smell of Crayola crayons takes many of us on a nonstop trip back to childhood. Who (apart from Yale University researchers) knows that the smell of crayons rank at number 18 among the 20 most recognizable smells in the United States—with coffee and peanut butter coming in at first and second?

Over the last 100 years, more than 600 shades of Crayola crayons have been produced. Time for focus. In June 1990, the owners of Crayola, Binney & Smith, decided to retire some of the older colors and replace them with brighter, sharper ones. This was a sensible, rational decision responding to the changing environment our kids live in. TV shows, clothing, toys—vibrant color showcases every one.

"Not so fast," said a band of Crayola fans. Calling themselves RUMPS (the Raw Umber and Maize Preservation Society, after two trashed tints), they picketed Crayola HQ. RUMPS was joined by another angry group: CRAYON (Committee to Re-establish All Your Old Norms).

Knowing Loyalty Beyond Reason when they saw it, Crayola quickly backed down and re-released the old colors in a special commemorative collection!

And Crayola has sometimes bowed too low to the spirit of the time. Like when they replaced the memorable "Flesh" with the bland "Peach." Or when they decided to rename Indian Red, and went to consumers for suggestions. Great idea, but sadly they chose "Chestnut" ahead of the two top runners-up, the intriguing "Baseball Mitt Brown" and the fantastic "The Crayon Formerly Known As Indian Red."

In 2003, Crayola was back on the retirement trail, asking the public to "save a shade." Five were on the block, one to be saved. Inspirational Consumer Jodi on www.iwilldare.com explained:

"The five colors up for ousting are Burnt Sienna, Blizzard Blue, Mulberry, Teal Blue, and Magic Mint. Yes, Magic Mint—what in the hell color is Magic Mint? And really, blizzards aren't blue, so that should automatically disqualify Blizzard Blue from staying. What will happen to scenes of autumn days if Burnt Sienna is ousted? What about horses? Brown-haired people? Bridges, log cabins, amber waves of grain? None of these will be possible without Burnt Sienna. Raw Umber will not do. Brown is too basic. Bittersweet doesn't cut it. We need Burnt Sienna. So my friends, I beg of you—help me save Burnt Sienna. Log on to Crayola.com and vote to save Burnt Sienna.

Thank you, Jodi.
(feel free to pass this on)"

The senses of the world

Our senses remind us who we are—what feels safe and familiar. The texture of both hominy grits and Molokhiyya, the Arab soup, are an offense to many palettes. The Japanese find the extravagant arm gestures of Europeans alarming. Spices that leave serious burns on some lips bring only a mild sweat to a Mumbai curry aficionado. A quick search of Google shows you that the Inuit apparently have distinct words for many different types of snow that would all look the same to me.

KATIKSUNIK light snow	ANIU snow packed hard	ILUQ thin snow on a window	POKAKTOK snow that looks like salt
APUT snow on ground	MASSAK watery snow	AKILLUKKAK soft snow	SILLIK hard icy snow
MILIK soft snow	SISUUK avalanche	PUKAK snow that looks like sugar	KATIKSUGNIK snow light enough to walk in
IMALIK falling wet snow	SULLARNIQ snow blown in	APUN snow	APINGAUT first snowfall
QANIIT snow in air	NITTAALAQ snow thick in the air	AYAK snow that has fallen on clothes	APUTITAQ patch of snow
KANNIK snowflake	NUTAGAK snow like powder	APIRLAAT snow that has just fallen	KAIYUGLAK snow in ripples
PERKSERTOK drifting snow	ANIUK snow to use as water	APUSINIQ snow in a drift	MIULIK sleet

Virgin

Richard Branson has got to be one of the great sensualists of our time.

The only big place I buy music from is Virgin. (The best "small" place is Hear, in Seattle–try it.) With their in-store headset stations, Virgin was the first to let me listen to the music I wanted to hear, not the music some punk happened to be playing.

Virgin Atlantic is a triumph of the senses. From the music room in the Upper-Class lounge to the totally cool reclining seats in the cabin. I have seen grown adults spend 20 minutes playing around with the seats, raising and lowering the plush red recliners. And then there are the massages, the facials, the bar.

And as for in-flight shopping, Virgin goes past the spirits, cigs, and perfume formula with a very savvy collection of stuff. And how do they group them? Right, by the senses.

On a clear day you can see forever.

Sight is a wonder. Our eyes absorb an incredible amount of information, and they do it fast. Little wonder that processing all this information takes up something like two-thirds of our cerebral cortex.

The fact is that humans think in images, not words. Try saying "TIGER" to a friend and ask her what she saw in her mind's eye. It won't be the letters T-I-G-E-R, I can tell you that.

No, she will have seen an image of orange and black stripes. That is why all memory courses use images and visual stories to help people remember stuff.

The born-again checked pattern from Burberry has become a worldwide luxury cult. From outfitting the military and intrepid explorers last century, Burberry has morphed into a high fashion staple. The streets of New York, Tokyo, Frankfurt, London or Sydney wouldn't be the same without that trademark red, camel, black and white check. It's their powerful visual signature of quality.

Easy to see, easy to read.

Putumayo World Music also has a distinctive visual style. The bold graphics on all of their CD covers are created by Nicola Heindl. In her work, the traditional and the contemporary meet, just as they do in Putumayo's music. Dan Storper explains:

"I bought a greeting card that Nicola had designed when I was in England 12 years ago. By coincidence, a friend of hers, Susan Brynner, was the display director for our retail stores, and she noticed the card on my bulletin board. She mentioned that Nicola was coming over from London and asked if I'd like to meet her. I was very interested, particularly because I'd already decided to start a CD series and thought her style would work well. Nicola agreed to create the first covers, and we've developed a long-term exclusive agreement for commercial products since then. We are currently planning a series of products utilizing her artwork, including culturally-themed note cards, travel journals, calendars, and books."

"Mommy, what color is the universe?"

In 2002, a couple of astronomers from Johns Hopkins University announced a massive turnaround. The universe, they announced, was not pale turquoise, as they had previously stated. **The universe was beige.** Karl Glazebrook and Ivan Baldry had been tripped up by a bug in their software, and Karl confessed all. "This is embarrassing but this is science. We are not like politicians. If we make mistakes we admit them. That's how science works."

They may be scientists, but these guys know the power of a good name. They figured "beige" was not going to do it and turned to their colleagues.

The top ten suggestions from other Johns Hopkins astronomers were:

Cappuccino Cosmico, Cosmic Cream, Astronomer Green, Astronomical Almond, Skyvory, Univeige, Cosmic Latté, Big-Bang Buff/Blush/Beige, Cosmic Khaki, Primordial Clam Chowder.

Paint it black

In New Zealand, where my home is, the color **black** has almost religious connotations. Here, **black** is the color of **passion**. The color of **commitment**. And the color of **victory**. New Zealanders **bleed black**.

The legendary **All Blacks** started it. They wear **black** boots, socks, pants, and shirts. Some say they come to games in mourning for their opponents.

And the spirit is infectious. Other New Zealand teams include the **Tall Blacks** (basketball) and the **Black Caps** (cricket).

For years there have been calls to change the present New Zealand flag. I am right behind it. From the British Union Jack and the four stars of the Southern Cross to a **black** flag crossed with New Zealand's famous silver fern. The true representation of New Zealand's spirit.

Ground control

Color is a billion-dollar business, and Pantone is out front
controlling it. I get to see a lot of designers, and they all share one tool.
The Pantone color range. Although Pantone has now moved over to on-line
color matching, the unmistakable bulky swatches are still to be found in shelves, on
desks, and next to screens all over the world.

Pantone writes the new language of color. Thousands of colors, sorted, graded, and named.
Thousands of colors matched around the globe.

I understand consistency and clarity is crucial for manufacturers, but the level of control
bothers me. I guess as the range gets more and more minutely differentiated, it becomes
unwieldy and we are kind of back to where we started.

Pantone, like the folks at the United States-based Color Marketing Group, are also into the
color prediction business.

When I addressed a Color Marketing Group conference, I learned that one of the purposes of
the Conference was to predict the future hot colors.

The extended concept-to-design-to-manufacturing cycle for many manufacturers demands that
color choices may have to be made up to three years ahead of marketing.

Who wants to be the sucker who launches the orange car in a world where blue stripes rule?

What I liked about their process was its weight on gut feeling and intuition. Much of the hard
work was done by groups of people getting together and sharing experiences.

Heart on fire

One person who has probably heard more about Lovemarks than is good for her is my wife, Rowena. From the first time we met at Mary Quant in the 60s, to our hectic life today, she has always understood the power of emotions. As an insider and a consumer, who better than Ro to talk to the Lovemarks of beauty?

"Working for Mary Quant gave me a lifelong Love of the fashion industry, and the wonderful years that Kevin and I lived in the Middle East gave me a crash course in touching the senses. Amazing tastes, overpowering sounds, evocative scents, and dramatic colors.

"Red is one of my favorites. I love its warmth and the hint of danger it always brings to the party. Red lipstick, with its incredible range from hot flame to the palest of pinks, has got to be one of a woman's most powerful allies.

"M·A·C's special understanding of the subtle power of color is a big part of why this brand is a Lovemark for me. Such a smart combination of intimacy and provocation. I worked for a time at the UN in Geneva so when M·A·C launched a 60s retro-colors range called Peacenik, I knew it was just for me. And M·A·C has celebrated the anniversary of another icon, the Playboy bunny, with a special limited-edition lipstick. How cool is that?

"My other beauty Lovemark is Olay. I've used it for years, and I'm a dedicated fan. Olay is simply part of the way I take care of myself and my skin. For always. I can hardly believe the price for such quality and all the development that has gone into Olay over the decades. And a breakthrough product like Regenerist means Botox need never knock at my door.

"Mary Quant is back in my life again after a visit to a hip department store in Tokyo last year. When I saw the familiar daisy logo on a range of stunning new fashion merchandise, my heart missed a beat. I snapped up a handbag and several T-shirts....If it hadn't been for the competition from dozens of Japanese girls, I might have bought out the store!"

Sounds good to me

Maybe it all started with Champagne, but there is something about drinks and sound that makes your mouth water. A water fountain splashing, the coffeemaker bubbling.

Fabio Fernandes and his F/Nazca Saatchi & Saatchi team in Brazil sold a beer for a client on a simple sound–the "*tssss*" of a cap coming off a bottle. Beer drinkers simply mouthed "*tssss*" to be served a chilled Brahma in any bar.

Of course Champagne producers have known about this connection for centuries.

The pop of a Champagne cork is one of the most evocative sounds in the Western world.

Yes, we all know it's not supposed to pop, but who can give up that extravagance and the anticipation?

I love music. No big surprise there. I make presentations all around the world, and to get the ideas flowing I use a song title or lyric as my inspiration.

Music has become the soundtrack of our lives. We attach songs to special moments and are flooded with memories when the right tune comes wafting by. And it's not just the music that plays this powerful role. The lyrics too give us phrases that can set our course in life, rally armies, bind lovers even closer together.

Music is important to us because it can set moods and trigger powerful emotions. We have always known this anecdotally, but we also know that anecdote is like a red flag to science. And so, in 1995, Jaak Panksepp, an intrepid neuroscientist from Bowling Green State University in Ohio, set out to put the anecdotes to the test. He asked several hundred young men and women why music was important to them.

Emotion turned out not only to be an answer, it was pretty much the answer.

Around 70 percent of both sexes said that music was important to them because "it elicits emotions and feeling." The next choice, a very distant second, was music's ability to "alleviate boredom."

For Lovemarks, the well-worn phrases—the voice of the product, the voice of the consumer, the voice of our time—are to be taken literally. Hearing and speaking are two of the most powerful forces in creating deep emotional connections with anyone. And you need them both. To speak without listening is to badger and hector. To listen and not speak is to lose your personality, and the conversation peters out.

Brands are already into sound—and I'm not just talking full-production TV commercials. Retail environments, phone messages, brand signatures, radio, and the Internet. At Toyota they are even interested in the silences!

"With the Prius we talk about quietness. Now noise can be measured by figures, but there is also a quietness that you feel with your body. For instance, with regard to the acceleration, the Prius is very different from other cars. You can time the speed of acceleration with a stopwatch, but the actual speed and the body's perception of it are very different. Of course, we do measure these things, and we set some target figures. But just because we get the target figure we are after, it doesn't mean it's okay. Figures are figures. We need to be able to *feel* the quietness or feel good about the acceleration as we actually experience it in the car. I think these things are very important."

[Masao Inoue, Chief Engineer, Product Planning Division, Toyota Motor Corporation]

Eye of the storm

My New York apartment is a sensual haven. In New Zealand, my family and I live in a beautiful piece of native bush, with tropical palms and 150-year-old kauri trees. So our house there connects directly to the landscape.

In New York—much as I love the place—the idea was to disconnect. Here, I live in the hurly-burly, working with 7,000 other souls worldwide in a whirlwind of emotional tension. I wanted to go back to a home that would be secure and warming, calming and relaxing—to an article of faith. I wanted to open the door into something uncomplicated. I wanted the feeling of being embraced.

Architect Sam Trimble responded to my brief with empathy and intelligence:

"I went to geology texts and an encyclopedia to find metaphors for how to define the space physically and conceptually. In my research, I learned about tectonic caves—

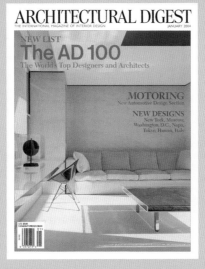

natural caverns that look ordered and structured—and I decided to create a space that seemed hollowed out, as though carved from solid rock."

Sam sourced a Portuguese limestone to transform the apartment into a cave. Its surface is variegated, hewn by its ancient geological history of shells and liquid flows. When I walk about in my bare feet, it is quiet and tactile. It caresses my soles!

Other natural materials were used throughout. The stone of the walls and floors is relieved by the softness of wood, and both are illuminated by plays of light and shadow.

Sam created such a beautiful, sensuous space that I didn't even need art on the walls.

I just walk in, and the space, its colors and surfaces, wrap and quiet me. The tranquillity liberates me. I'm refreshed here. Though I'm far away from New Zealand, I feel at home.

Picking up the scent

The human senses of smell and taste are intertwined so tightly it is hard to experience one without the other. Bonded together they speak more directly than the rest to our emotions, our memories and our dreams. Smell dominates taste. While humans have four genes for vision, there are over 1,000 allocated to smell.

With around 400,000 recognizable odors in the world, we have access to an incredible storehouse of potential connections.

They say that smell is almost exclusively stored in the long-term memory. Why else was Marcel Proust's most famous memory-jog the taste of a small cake, not its shape or name?

I remember a friend telling me a great story about the power of smell. She'd been trying to sell her house with no luck for a couple of months. When she changed agents, the new one suggested baking cookies in the oven just before people came to look over the house. The effect was immediate. The first people to visit signed up.

The association of the warm, cozy scent of cookies in the oven turned the house into a home.

"If you were to say, 'Name a brand that has managed to get big fast, make quality products, treat its people very well and respectfully, and understand the differences in economies and tastes in other parts of the world, while continuing to grow,' one brand that comes to my mind is Starbucks. Part of what's interesting about Starbucks is the extent to which they define what they're producing not as a cup of coffee, but rather a wonderful experience, a break, a chance for some community and relationship-building. Their stores create this third space for people in the middle of the rush and crush of everyday life. They're not selling coffee, and they know it. They're selling something much more emotional. I was joking to somebody that in the old days you'd take your coffee to the office. Now with Wi-Fi at Starbucks, you take your office to the coffee. That's an amazing success."

[Alan Webber, Founding Editor, *Fast Company*]

Whether Starbucks plays mostly on taste or smell is up for debate. This extraordinary business has built a veritable empire on the experience of a hard brown bean. By making sure that the aroma of coffee infused their cafes, Starbucks created a distinctive place that their consumers loved to be in. And everyone else has noticed.

The retail world is being transformed as the potential of the senses is realized.

We are entering the samplers' paradise. The favorite hang-out of the sensualist. Soaps, baked goods, and paints are allowed to smell exactly as they are. Suddenly it is okay for a fish market to smell like…a fish market.

As far as taste goes, it is now hard to believe that the much-loved Japanese snack, sushi, was once thought of in the West as cold, wet fish wrapped in seaweed. The Lovemark lesson? Don't knock tastes because you don't like them the first time round. Red Bull doesn't appeal to me, but millions of people love it.

They don't call F1 fans 'petrol-heads' for nothing. What a sensual extravaganza Formula One racing has become! High-octane fumes, the vibration of engines, the acrid smell of burning rubber. Overpowering. Put one percent of that energy into any other business and you've got a sensation on your hands. No wonder sensation and Sensuality are members of the same family.

Every one of us has a personal odor that's as distinctive as a fingerprint. Why then have businesses been so shy about using this most sensual of the senses?

Why do so few corporations have their own scent?

My thought is that smell is so direct, so personal, and so specific, that people back off messing with it. This is why you break open the game if you get it right.

My heart in my mouth

In the past decade we have learned more about the five basic taste qualities–sour, sweet, salty, bitter, and the recently described umami*–than we did in the previous 2,000 years.

We are at the dawning of a taste revolution.

The exploration of taste (and smell as the larger part of it) is now a huge part of Research and Development. The hitch is that, of all the senses, taste remains the most difficult to measure. It is deeply subjective. It's tough to work out the elements of a flavor where the quantities are so minute.

Science's solution? Taste scientists roam the globe searching for new tastes and novel ingredients. They hunt them, locate them, trap them, and then they take their treasures home to analyze and recreate them in the laboratory.

And yet the biggest challenge remains. How can you predict what people will like? Try going "out" from human emotion rather than "in" from chemistry. Taste and smell are huge opportunities in the creation of Lovemarks. Both are pretty well limited to the food and fragrance industries today.

To think to yourself:

"What is the taste of that car?" or
"How does this DVD player smell?" seems silly.

Time to get over that response. Expanding the senses into organizations, into product development, into consumer relationships can be a fantastic inspiration and a potential game-breaker.

*The word umami is derived from *umai*, the Japanese word for "delicious." More elusive than the Big Four, it is often described as "meaty" or "brothy."

My favorite example is Apple's wonderful campaign for the iMac. They took taste out of the mouth and into the heart with their iMac advertisements. They made their computers in shades of strawberry, grape, and blueberry. And the message? YUM!

Pure Lovemark thinking. Apple customers are famously Loyal Beyond Reason. They really do think their computers are good enough to eat.

At Saatchi & Saatchi, we are using Lovemarks to focus on Sensuality. Take a campaign we did for Procter & Gamble and their anti-dandruff shampoo Head & Shoulders. In bus shelters, we featured an image of a young woman with the wind in her hair. People were invited to press a button to activate a puff of citric-scented mist.

The memory of this scent and its association with a fresh, free spirit is what endures.

That magic touch

Fact: The skin is the largest organ in the body. **Fact:** The human skin has a special network of nerves. **Fact:** Our fingertips, tongue, and lips have the most nerve endings.

So where do we go from there?

With our fingertips we can instantaneously identify smooth, rough, hard, soft, wet, dry, hot, and cold through tightly packed nerve endings. Put that sensitivity together with muscles and joints that tell us how much force we are applying or is pressed against us, and we can get intense sensations from just about anything we come in contact with.

No wonder that when things are going well we talk about *feeling* good.

There are some places that do touch so well they become inspirations for the rest of us. Italy has got to be top of the list. Arrive at an Italian airport and you know you're deep in the land of the embrace. There have been serious academic studies of whether Italians touch more than everyone else. The conclusion? They do. Italians were never taught "don't touch!" and their superbly tactile design heritage springs straight from these sensitive hands.

That's the way it goes with touch. Even when everyone is wrong, everyone is also right.

Consider the Indian parable about the six blind men and the elephant.

The first blind man reached out and touched the side of the huge animal. "The elephant," he said, "is nothing but a wall." The second man felt the elephant's trunk. "The elephant," he concluded, "is most likely related to the snake family." The third blind man, chancing on the tusk, declared the elephant to be sharp and deadly like a spear. As he grabbed hold of the elephant's tail, the fourth blind man was convinced the elephant was like a piece of rope. The fifth man, feeling the ear, declared the elephant to be like a fan. As he put his arms around the elephant's massive legs, the last blind man scoffed at the others. "It is obvious," he said. "The elephant is exactly like a tree."

Why are most of the textures in cars so similar? Shut your eyes. Are there any distinctive clues to the brand? Occasionally there might be a how-boring-is-that leather/wood mix or (in the cheaper models) a don't-worry-about-me-I'm-just-the-driver vinyl/plastic combo.

"The feel of a car often comes down to the small things, like the feel when you actually touch the material, leather, or wood. This is a new kind of thinking, thinking of how things feel to the consumer. To make my decisions, I must always ride in the car. There are many things that you cannot find from data that you discover when you ride in a car. There is nothing, no machine, that can replace the human body. It is the best sensor. For example, when you turn the steering wheel, sometimes you can just feel a sound. So faint you can't really measure it, but the feel of it is there. Also, things like the glove box, the console box, or the cup holder. When you open and close them they create their own sounds. And there are often faint sounds that can really irritate the person who is driving a car. The aim is to create a stillness that you can't actually measure by figures in the normal sense, and this is done by feeling and touch."

[Masao Inoue, Chief Engineer, Product Planning Division, Toyota Motor Corporation]

Where does the auto industry put its major investment? Into reducing touch, with power steering, super-suspension, state-of-the-art tires. No wonder we end up feeling like the boy in the bubble! Out of touch. Literally.

We need touch back. A new challenge for the might of mass production matched by the invention of technologies that use touch.

I have watched with fascination as kids have responded enthusiastically to tactile experiences in game controllers. Take the Xbox controller. Eight buttons, two triggers, three toggling switches… and untapped possibilities.

No wonder the under-25 set in Japan calls itself "The Thumb Generation." Mobile text-messaging marks a divide between generations that is as clear-cut as the flares/no flares debate.

There is serious sense behind the idea of touchpoints with consumers. Every business is starting to realize this. From the supermarket shelf and the coupon book to the TV spot, the mailer, and all points in between, touching people matters.

In our determination to make life easier we have removed valuable sources of sensation from many products. Beating clothes against a stone has nothing much to recommend it, but I'm not so sure dropping them into a machine and pushing a button is the complete answer either. Somewhere in the middle there is an important place for our precious senses.

1. Lead with your senses. Approach everything you do with all five senses on high alert. If it doesn't cuddle up to at least two or three of your senses, ask why not.

2. Come up with an idea for how each of the five senses connects with your brand. No cheating! Five senses, five ideas. Test them with your colleagues and with the first 10 consumers you meet.

3. Establish the sensory priorities of your brand. Where are you strong? Where do you have work to do? Create a visual representation of your plan.

4. Make music a priority. Surprise your next group meeting with unexpected sound. Hijack the sound system in the elevator.

5. Revere great design. Share your favourite examples, from CD covers to stationery to the latest mobile phone or even new vegetables!

Five things
to do tomorrow

Chapter 10

CLOSE TO YOU

What can turn an experience that is given to thousands and thousands of people into a meaningful one for you? Intimacy.

The big question for me has always been, how do you get intimate with consumers without being invasive or insincere?

My question was answered on a Qantas flight to New Zealand. I was tired and distracted as I got on board. All I wanted was to get to my seat, put away my bag, and sit down. When a flight attendant stepped in front of me, I admit I was only halfway pleased to see him. He smiled politely, and asked, "Can I get you a Chardonnay, sir?…Or a beer, mate?" That's how you do Intimacy.

As we developed Lovemarks at Saatchi & Saatchi, Mystery and Sensuality were our immediate focus. They showed us big, new, and exciting ways that would help people reconnect with brands in a deeper and more emotionally satisfying way.

But as we moved in deeper we began to realize that something was missing. A still, quiet voice. A voice that talked not about big effects or sensations, but about the minutiae of everyday life.

Personal. Sensitive. Continuous. What we were missing was Intimacy.

Sure we need thrills, spills, and big gestures in our relationships, but we also need closeness, trust, and (you've got it) Intimacy.

Because Intimacy touches directly on our personal aspirations and inspirations, it is much more contentious than Mystery and Sensuality. It pushes up close to what sort of relationships we want to have; the kinds of families we need, what we share, what we don't, who sets the boundaries.

Intimacy poses questions like: How close can I get to you and still feel comfortable? How much do I want you to know about me? How much do I want to know about you?

People of different cultures and at different times have treated Intimacy very differently. We know for instance that the friendly handshake that starts so many greetings had its beginnings in the wary exposure of hands without knives or other weapons—another age's version of the airport frisk!

The three-cheek kiss of the French, the hongi nose-press of New Zealand Māori, the New Age hug, the high-five of the street. They all show very different faces of Intimacy.

Close up

A crucial problem for brands in their battle against commodification is their growing apart from consumers. Distant, undifferentiated, unremarkable.

Focused on growth and clamoring for attention, brands don't have a lot of time for nuance and sensitivity. I'll amend that—no time at all.

McDonald's and Nike and the rest of the U.S.-created, global front-runners are struggling to retain the emotional ties that have made them legends and billion-dollar businesses.

The big question: Have the brands themselves changed? Or is it the other way around? Has what people want from brands changed?

My take on the brand/consumer relationship digs deep into the patterns of human behavior. Look back at the 1950s and 60s and the place the automobile had in the hearts of the American public. It was in so close that to have a family photograph without the family wagon as backdrop made no sense at all. Fast-forward to the 21st century.

When was the last time you
lined up in front of the family
car and took a picture?

People need Intimacy in their lives. But businesses have let many already well-defined opportunities slip away.

Many of the big brands became standoffish over the 1990s. Removing themselves from the people who gave them their life–consumers– they fixed on another audience: shareholders.

What a shareholder demands
of a brand is very, very different
from what's demanded by
someone who loves it.

Shareholders very seldom love the brands they have invested in. And the last thing they want is an intimate relationship. They figure this could warp their judgement. They want measurability, increasing returns (always), and no surprises (ever). Imagine a relationship with someone like that!

No wonder so many brands lost the emotional thread that had led them to their extraordinary success and turned them instead into metric-munchers of the lowest kind. Watch for the sign: **Heads, not hearts, at work here.**

They forget all about the intimate dimension of relationships. They loved Customer Relationship Management. They honed their skills assessing the benefits from sponsorships, entertainment partnerships, and all the other "ships." But if you attempted to get up close… they dashed to the other side of the board-room table. They ignored the power of Intimacy. They neglected to look at the intimate responses that illuminate the great Lovemarks.

So many Lovemarks have pet names it could almost be a prerequisite.

Gimme a Bud.
Who owns that Jag?
We're going to Harvey Nicks...
or Bloomies,
depending on where you live.

I'll have a Coke.

Federal Express got it. They understood this kind of Intimacy was a gift–and shortened their name.

FedEx it to me....

Transact a Love affair? I don't think so.

Intimacy was crushed over the 20th century. Everyone was determined to reduce complex exchanges of buying and selling into fast and efficient transactions. Little wonder that the people visiting the mall figured something was missing from their lives. Where once the moment of choice was wrapped in an intimate relationship with the seller, it has often become a sterile experience in an aisle that stretches forever.

"As a rule of thumb, if the guy who asks you to pick a card, any card, is wearing a top hat, he's not giving you a real choice."

[Penn Jillette, magician, of Penn & Teller]

Shoppers respond by getting the hell out as fast as they can. On an average supermarket visit, they are now spending only 32 minutes doing their major weekly shopping.

Now there's nothing wrong with streamlining or with efficiency. Everyone wants to save time and dollars whether they are a shopper, a manufacturer, a truck driver.

But why throw your heart out the window with the numbers?

Anyone who has been to the Tsukiji fish market in Tokyo knows what I am talking about. Tuna auctions where millions of dollars of frozen fish are sold without a computer or calculator in sight.

I am not suggesting that business go back to handshakes and scraps of paper, but there is a lot to learn from the intimate network of trust that the traditional marketplace thrives on.

As the mass market geared up, businesses lost their way. They became detached from personal relationships.

Everyone with a telephone has had a total stranger (aka telemarketer) asking how they are and did they have a nice day. As if they cared. Bank tellers and supermarket checkout staff treat us as long-lost friends. Our first names–formerly the province of friends and family–have become common currency. E-mail spam is simply part of this trend…on steroids.

And what is the result? It feels all wrong. Trouble is that all this,

"Hi! I'm Harry, I'll be your best friend for this evening"

is based on process and careful targeting and not on intimate knowledge. They presume too much. And human beings can spot that sort of falseness fast. Real fast.

But connect with people's emotions and–despite all their concerns about privacy–they will tell you almost anything. A Jupiter research project once found that 82 percent of all respondents would give personal information to a new shopping site so they could enter a $100 sweepstake!

The trick is not to exploit this thirst for personal connections, but to slake it with integrity.

Two-way street

While Intimacy is fundamental to sustaining emotional connections, it is more elusive than Mystery and Sensuality. Why? Because Intimacy has got to be a two-way process. Listening as well as talking.

Listening is something that most brands are not great at. They evolved alongside the mass media, and that is where most of them have stayed. Talking, talking, talking.

The fragmentation of media demands a fresh approach. And this is where Lovemarks come in. Not to abandon the mass market, but to transform it with multiple emotional connections.

Intimacy requires an understanding of what matters to people at a very deep level. And that understanding means that you have to be prepared to reveal yourself as well. Reveal your true feelings.

Not standard behavior for most corporations!

But this is where we need to venture.

Lovemarks are owned by the people who love them.

Not by the companies and people who design, produce, market, and distribute them. To act in the knowledge that consumers own Lovemarks calls for radical change. And one of the most radical is opening up to Intimacy. It is only through Intimacy that the barriers of reserve will dissolve and brands can become Lovemarks.

Some brands seem to be intimate almost without trying. Oprah Winfrey is a spellbinding example. Her mix of no-nonsense advice and personal insight is a formula that has worked for a number of talk show hosts.

But then, just when everyone thought the idea had rung all its changes, Oprah added a new dimension. Intimacy.

Oprah understands the power of Intimacy as well as anyone I have ever seen on television. She also understands how this Intimacy can transform lives.

The camera loves Oprah Winfrey, but instead of loving it back like other talk show hosts, she looks right through it and connects directly with her audience. That's Oprah's secret. Transformation, not just communication.

> "I'm interested in helping women create intimacy in their lives and in their relationships. Once you have reached a certain level of maturity, whether you are 28 or 48, you understand that 50 orgasms a minute does not exist."
>
> [Oprah Winfrey]

The challenge of one

Intimacy will meet a tough new challenge in the coming decades: the single-person household. And traditional ways of dealing with people as members of coherent groups is just not going to play.

Humans cannot live without intimate relationships, and yet we seem to be constructing a world where Intimacy is harder and harder to achieve. And we are going crazy doing it.

On CNN I saw a recent poll in which American singles said that what they most missed from not being in a relationship was companionship. And then I read that a whole bunch of people in America felt that watching "Friends" on TV was part of their social life. Give me a break.

Walking the streets around my apartment in TriBeCa, I am astonished at the number of women I see walking large dogs.

At first I thought the dogs were for protection. Now I realize they offer true companionship. And it's not just an American condition.

By the year 2010, some 40 percent of households will belong to "home alone" single people. "Single living" will be most visible among those of younger middle-age. It is those who are now in their late 20s or early 30s who are predicted to want to go it alone.

A new global trend—the rising number of singles

- In 1950, about 3 percent of the population of Europe and the United States lived alone. Today in the U.K., seven million adults live alone—three times as many as 40 years ago. The statistics bible *Social Trends* estimates that by 2020 one-person households will make up 40 percent of total households.
- In France, the number of people living on their own has more than doubled since 1968.
- About 40 percent of Swedes now live alone.
- The shift towards solo living is most pronounced in the big urban centers of the West—with over 50 percent of households in Munich, Frankfurt, and Paris containing just one person, while in London nearly four in ten people live on their own.
- Since 1960, the number of German 25- to 45-year-olds living on their own has risen by 500 percent.
- The growth in single-person households is mainly a result of an increasing number of 25s to 45s opting to live alone.

Intimacy has three very different faces:

- **Empathy, so that we can understand and respond to other people's emotions**
- **Commitment, which proves that we are in the relationship for the long haul**
- **Passion, that bright spark that keeps the relationship alive**

Empathy

There is only one way to understand other people's emotions, or to really understand anything for that matter. By listening.

In my experience, empathy is most often created out of language and the silences that surround it. When do you hear the most astonishing insights? When you create an emotionally powerful space for them to settle into, by listening.

Empathy is created out of the tension between the sound of the voice and an intended silence.

As we quickly find out when we enter intimate relationships, what is said is often not so important. It is the inflections, the pauses, the combination of sounds and body language. This creates a complex mix of signs and signals that builds an empathetic relationship.

Marketers find this very hard to accept. Their disciplines are founded on rational analysis and conclusions, not idle chat and unfinished sentences. In their goal to push as much information as possible, marketers fail consistently to make real connections. Intimacy is an understanding of what we are sharing in this moment, not just what is being communicated.

Quick flings become lifelong Love affairs through empathy. Without empathy you can't do emotion, you can't do Intimacy– and you can forget all about truthful and transforming consumer insights.

I have always claimed Toyota's Camry is a Lovemark. And it is not just because the Camry has been the bestselling car in America so many times, year in and year out. It is because the Camry has extraordinary empathy with so many consumers.

The Camry is a quiet car that keeps to itself. It balances brilliantly on the cutting edge of normal. It doesn't go for the big splash, but it does everything required of it–and more. Sounds like a good friend or a family member. The ones who make you feel better just by being there. No dramas, no fuss, just solid support and understanding. They don't forget your birthday, they don't nag, and they always remember you love red roses.

Love comes in many shapes. One of the strongest is the enduring Love built on intimate understanding. Camry owners know this.

They have fallen in Love with a car that understands they don't want to attract attention. A car that knows Love can be a private experience. That it doesn't have to hold hands and kiss in the street. So let's not forget this Love that binds. Camry hasn't.

Another kind of engine, Google, has taken its own route to empathy, and been well rewarded for it. Google says it deals to more than 150 million searches a day. While engines like Yahoo! turned into a system of portals, Google kept it simple. Very simple. So simple that the temporary addition of a Christmas tree felt like a major statement. You want empathy? How about your consumers loving what you do so much they invent a new expression based on your brand name–"to Google"!

A moving experience

Rethink the mobile phone. Yes, I know all the stuff about interrupting concerts, distracted drivers putting lives in danger, loud talkers annoying everyone else in a restaurant, but mobile phones can teach us a very different lesson about what people value as well.

Let's go back to the beginning.

The telephone has a strange history. The initial concept was as a broadcast machine. One person could talk to many others far away via telephone lines. And perhaps play a little music. Well, that didn't work! It is in our blood to talk back.

The telephone then found its true calling as an instrument of personal communication. As someone born in England, I have always been amused by the role the class system there played in holding up the diffusion of this cool new technology.

It seems that many people point-blank refused to use the telephone because they might have to speak with someone to whom they had had no formal introduction! Can't get less intimate than that.

The telephone survived the stupidity of snobbery and opened up a whole new world of Intimacy. People could keep in touch. They could swap confidences in a way they would never think of in face-to-face encounters. They could make their lives faster and easier.

In the 1990s the mobile phone took the transformation of everyday life to another level altogether—constant communication. As the yuppie label faded rapidly, the mobile phone became an instrument of Intimacy. The builder of relationships.

If you want to be empathetic, you would have to admit there is a hell of a lot to listen to.

In an average day an adult can use as many as 40,000 words. That's about five hours of continuous speech. If you multiply this by an average age of 75, that's over a billion words in a lifetime.

And what will all these words be about? Important issues of the day? Very, very few of them. Most of our talk could be termed trivial. It's about the process of talking rather than the content. We talk about family and friends, the weather, local news, and (especially) the day's goings-on. Gossip is the lifeblood of Intimacy.

People now automatically phone home to announce they are in the car and on the way home. Everyone is constantly calling everyone else to explain where they are, what is happening, what might happen. A point-by-point tracking throughout our lives with our loved ones.

Intimate talking has become a 24/7 activity. Forget grammar and argument. We're talking haphazard, incomplete, and emotional. This is not about communicating information as we have known it. This is a constant sensing of where you are, where I am, and how we are both feeling.

Commitment

To me commitment is one of the most important and most demanding of the Lovemark attributes. Remember that great definition of the difference between being committed and being involved? In a plate of bacon and eggs, the pig is committed, the chicken is just involved.

Long-term commitment—crucial to a Lovemark relationship.

Working with P&G, I was introduced to Cape Town academics Jan Hofmeyr and Butch Rice's *Commitment-Led Marketing*. We all agree that loyalty is not enough. As Hofmeyr and Rice point out, loyalty can just be consumers acting on autopilot, continuing to buy the same brand because they can't be bothered to make another choice.

Too tired to leave

But commitment can transform loyalty from an unthinking acceptance to a real state imbued with real emotion–Loyalty Beyond Reason.

This combination of loyalty and commitment is the powerful force we need to harness for Lovemarks. Getting to that crucial place where people are beyond the information stage and point-by-point comparisons. They have made their choice. They have committed to it before friends and family. It is part of them. And they are not going to change now.

Fan clubs are a sure sign you are in the Lovemarks zone. They're also a great way to test the intensity of feeling. Start with LEGO and LUGNET, the fan-created International LEGO Users Group Network. Not owned by LEGO, but captured by the LEGO experience.

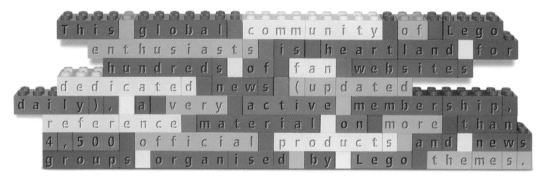

This global community of Lego enthusiasts is heartland for hundreds of fan websites dedicated news (updated daily), a very active membership, reference material on more than 4,500 official products and news groups organised by Lego themes.

From Adventurers to Robotics, Pirates to Football. They swap, sell, debate, argue, learn.

Fandom has gone up a notch with the onset of the Internet. We can now view thousands of movies starring the LEGO family. Check out www.geocities.co.jp/Hollywood/9060/cinemae.html for an unforgettable version of *The Matrix* or www.planetofthegeeks.com/workbench/lego/legomovies.html for something less sophisticated.

As for commitment of a different flavor, take Lucky Charms, the breakfast cereal with marshmallows. A clear Lovemark to millions of little kids throughout the United States. But Lucky Charms are also the Number One breakfast cereal consumed on college campuses!

Now that's serious commitment, when you get college kids eating the same cereal they loved as youngsters. And doing it in public. The cute message for this group of cereal lovers? "I got lucky at breakfast!"

Committed people are prepared to wait…and wait.

3 to 4 weeks
for a reservation at the Le Caprice restaurant in London.

Up to 1 month
for an underground tour of the Mt. Isa mine in Australia.

3 to 12 weeks
for a Padron Millennium cigar.

9 months
for a bouncing baby girl or boy.

6 to 18 months
for a Harley-Davidson Softail Deuce.

2 years
to join the Reebok Sports Club/NY, the world's most advanced fitness facility.

2 years
to receive treatments with the highly therapeutic Moor Mud in Austria, renowned for its healing properties.

Up to 2 years
for Aston Martin's V12 Vanquish.

2 to 3 years
to have your Japanese sword polished in Japan.

Around 3 years
in Singapore for Kelly and Birkin bags by Hermès.

5 years
for a Rolex Daytona watch.

Up to 5 years
to become one of the towns hosting a Tour de France start or finish.

18 years
for season tickets to the New York Giants.

25 years
for a 150-year-old wall-mounted GPO (General Post Office) box. With keys.

Loyalty Beyond Reason is what persuaded the Apple tribe to keep buying the brand when Apple was producing bland, beige boxes no different than any other on the market. For people who had joined Apple because it was cool, buying one of these computers was a big ask. Many of them stuck with it–all the time wondering why.

Steve Jobs made his triumphal return to Apple in 1994. Back on track, the company went to the leading edge and stayed there. And all those committed consumers felt vindicated. More loyal than ever. What sustained the Mac lovers over the tough beige period?

I call it "Love in the bank."

With Loyalty Beyond Reason, Apple could make mistakes and still be forgiven. This is the reward for a Lovemark. Only Love will get consumers through the bad times when common sense tells them they should change. Because Apple users loved the product, they were committed to it as an idea of themselves. They were Apple people. Loved members of the Apple family.

For Microsoft, looking down from the top of its multi-billion-dollar mountain, the Apple story may seem inconsequential. Big mistake. The lesson for Microsoft is not the threat of Apple building a bigger company based on Love and commitment, but Microsoft's own chances of retaining one that's not. Bigger giants than Microsoft have decayed. When something better and more lovable came along, nobody was committed enough to hang around.

Passion

There is one more thing that I believe Lovemarks need that aligns with Intimacy, empathy, and commitment. It is the intensity and rush that accompanies only the strongest emotions. Put together with Love it can transform the most insignificant product into a must-have. It has the power to give an intensity to a relationship that will carry it through good times and bad. Passion.

With passion, the most difficult of objectives can be achieved.

Without passion, the best-laid plans can wither and die. Analyzing it is a waste of time. Having it is a blessing and a gift.

When Nike signed up Michael Jordan, even they never suspected how passionately consumers would continue to feel about this man.

Clare Hamill, Vice President, Nike Goddess, says:

"The Brand Jordan phenomenon that's a part of the Nike brand continues to show an inexplicable Love for that man. With Michael Jordan, it's personal. You call him Michael, you have a name relationship with him. Somehow sports teams and some key athletes can really create that kind of emotional connection. They're like your family. You live and die if they do."

Passion can deepen if it can be handed on from person to person. The Zippo lighter has been an inspiration to American servicemen throughout the world. Why is this? Apart from the fact that the lighter works every time, I think it has to do with the way Zippo has encouraged the use of its lighter as a mini billboard. Having your Zippo engraved with a personal slogan has become a rite of passage for millions of soldiers and sailors.

It all started in the Second World War when U.S. soldiers, far from home, regarded their Zippos as prized possessions, often personalizing them with unique Trench Art. Ernie Pyle, the famous WWII war correspondent, wrote in August 1944:

"If I were to tell you how much these Zippos are coveted at the front, and the gratitude and delight with which the boys receive them, you would probably accuse me of exaggeration. I truly believe that the Zippo lighter is the most coveted thing in the army."

So why bother?

Letting consumers participate in the brand is very powerful. With Lovemarks, as with personal relationships, you often gain power by giving it away.

The obvious question is, of course, why should a business care whether its products are Lovemarks or not? After all, things are going pretty well for companies like Microsoft. Why should a father be generous to his kids? Why should we care about our next-door neighbors? Because that's how we create a world we love to live in. It's also how we create long-lasting relationships–and Loyalty Beyond Reason. Without Love, I guarantee even the greatest businesses will topple. They won't even see it coming because no one will care enough to tell them. It has happened before and will happen again. Even if you are the biggest, the best, or the brightest, why wouldn't you also crave to be the most loved? Why wouldn't you want to help make the world a better place?

1. Call three consumers. Every day. Chat about how they are doing, respond to their thoughts and ideas. Follow up. And then follow up some more.

2. Spread your email address around. Sure, you'll get some spam, but being open to the world is worth as much spam as you can eat.

3. Reinvent your vocabulary. Ask your colleagues for the words and phrases you use all the time. Do they suggest Mystery, Sensuality, or Intimacy — or the corporation?

4. For every decision you make, ask Who benefits? Is it the consumer? If not, focus on your decision for another 10 concentrated minutes and work out a way to change it.

5. Have you ever been invited to a customer's birthday party? If not, make that invitation your mission — or hold the party at your place!

Five things
to do tomorrow

Chapter 11

ACROSS
THE BORDER

The Love/Respect Axis

Saatchi & Saatchi's Chairman Bob Seelert is a smart man and a great sounding board for ideas that are struggling to realize themselves. We were waiting at Auckland Airport late one evening on our way to Los Angeles and I started on my Love rap. Bob had heard most of it before, but this time I pulled out a napkin and drew a horizontal line showing Love at one end and Respect at the other.

I showed Bob how it might work. How everything was telling us that brands had run out of juice. How they had to evolve into something more. And how I would place this new kind of brand near the Love end of the line. Lots of Respect, but moving towards high Love on the right. Products would stay at the far left, low Respect, low Love. The standard brands would probably be somewhere in the middle.

The goal would be at the head of the line. High on Love!

Bob looked at it for a couple of minutes. "There's another way to show this to more effect," he told me. Taking the pen he drew a second line, this one crossing over my Love/Respect line midway. My line was transformed in an instant into an axis.

And Bob was so right. The axis format immediately showed Love as a goal above and beyond Respect.

Now we could clearly show the ongoing importance of Respect and the urgency of moving into a relationship based on Love. Love of design, Love of service, Love of customers, Love of life.

Without Respect there is no foundation for any long-term relationship. Without the sharp delineation of the axis format, it was too easy for our ideas about Love to float off into feelings with no practical edge. Okay if we wanted to be psychotherapists about it, but somehow that was not where we were headed! Bob brought Love to earth.

Respect is the key to the success of many of our biggest clients. Such success should not be devalued; it's just no longer enough.

Companies like big-time Saatchi & Saatchi clients Toyota and Procter & Gamble have invested billions and won astonishing Respect for their products and brands. And they have done it through sustained feats of focus and self-discipline. Whatever we called the new generation of brands, it was going to need Respect–and a lot of it. Respect, it was clear, had to be tablestakes. No Respect, no admission.

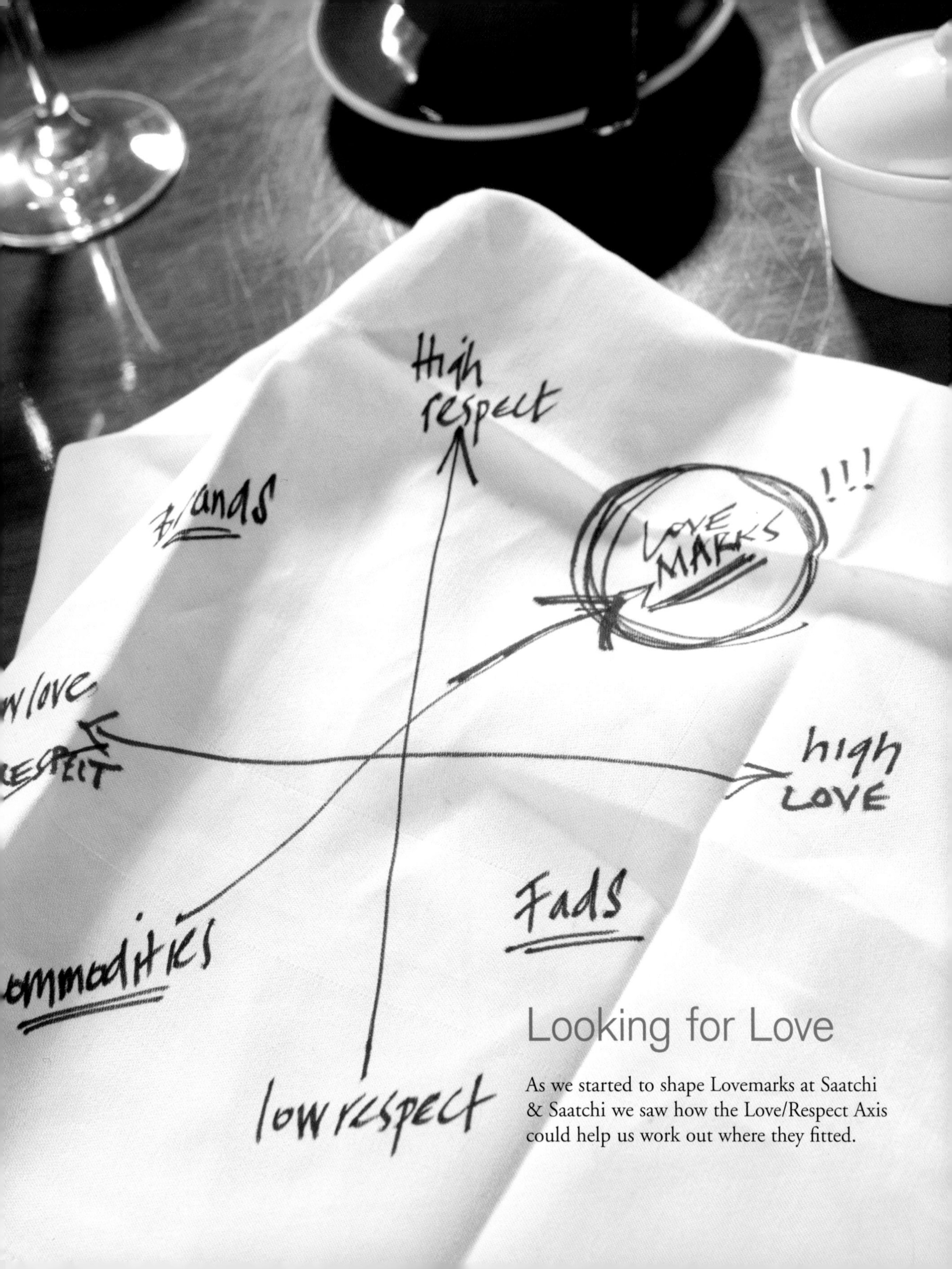

High
respect

Brands

Love
MARKS !!!

low love
RESPECT

high
LOVE

commodities

Fads

low respect

Looking for Love

As we started to shape Lovemarks at Saatchi & Saatchi we saw how the Love/Respect Axis could help us work out where they fitted.

How low
can you go?

It was obvious that the lower left-hand area–low Respect, low Love–would hold commodities. The products people need but don't desire, or even like a lot. Sand, iron, salt, gravel, that sort of stuff. Some of them make it out of the shade and work their way up. Basmati rice is one example. So is Carrara marble. Could brands fall from grace back into this commodification hole? Telcos will tell you the answer to that one. You bet they can.

After one of my presentations, a young marketer came up to me with an important question.

"You say emotion is the key to building relationships," she said. "I'm in the brick industry. How do you make bricks emotional?" "You don't," I told her. "But," I added, "what you do do is talk about what the bricks stand for: homes, families sitting around the fireplace feeling safe and warm. Achievements. Buildings built by bricklayers whose inspirational dream was nothing less than to touch the sky."

The bottom right-hand area had to be the home of fads, fashion, and infatuations. Loved for 15 minutes and then tossed aside to make way for the next cool item in the queue. From hula hoops to kipper ties* to "Survivor." Infatuations grow from our fantasies about who we are and where we belong. They thrive on hope, not understanding. Fun, frothy, and right for the moment. And just that moment. You can make a lot of money out of a fad, but your timing must be impeccable. Who wants a bunch of Beanie Babies now?

Some rare infatuations can transform into Love. Look at the Sony PlayStation. Initiated as a gaming system with Nintendo in 1991, Sony quickly went it alone and released the first PlayStation in Japan in 1994. It stormed past the established competition offered by Sega and Nintendo and took another leap forward with the release of the PlayStation2 in 2001. No one is calling it a fad any more.

*Don't remember those extra-wide kipper ties? That's because they were only a fad. Here today, forgotten tomorrow.

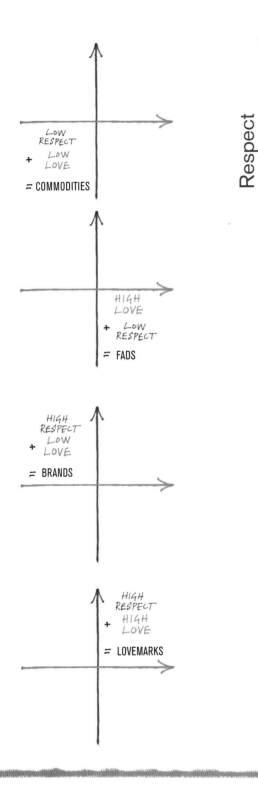

LOW
RESPECT
+ LOW
LOVE
= COMMODITIES

HIGH
LOVE
+ LOW
RESPECT
= FADS

HIGH
RESPECT
+ LOW
LOVE
= BRANDS

HIGH
RESPECT
+ HIGH
LOVE
= LOVEMARKS

Respect

Love

Stuck in the middle with you

Above the low Respect line on the left are most brands. This is where the efforts and investment of the last 50 years have gotten them. But many risk falling into the sand trap below, tough competition, tight margins, and lack of individuality turning them into "blands." Others have built up high levels of Respect based on sound management and continuous improvement. But what they have earned in Respect has little emotion. Sensible and well measured, it's hard to tell one from another.

The high life—Lovemarks

In the top right, the sun always shines: high Respect, high Love. Why wouldn't you want to be there? You know by instinct who belongs in this quadrant. Virgin is there. United would like to be. The iMac? Yes. The ThinkPad? Don't think so. It's home for Disneyland but not for Six Flags.

Make your own list.

The Love/Respect Axis is at its best in conversation: conversations about products and brands and what they need in order to become Lovemarks, conversations about successes, conversations to spark insights.

Jill Novak, a Saatchi & Saatchi Senior Vice President in New York, and Eric Lent, Kodak's Director of Youth Marketing, got together over the Love/Respect Axis to trace how Kodak got to grips with the youth market in the United States.

By the mid-1990s a new force was about to start snapping pictures: Generation Y. Kids born between 1979 and 1994.

Gen Y had the biggest discretionary spending power of any teen demographic in history. And they loved photography, particularly girls from 12 to 17.

The trouble was that Kodak was experiencing some keen competition from Fuji, and Gen Y's comfort with technology made the situation even more critical. Eric sums up the issue:

"Technology had never entered a generation's cultural vernacular in such an intense way. The category was heading away from traditional photography to digital photography, making these young consumers even more important. They were the ones to drive the adoption of new products and services. We absolutely had to alter their perceptions of us and create a relationship that could last a lifetime."

For a company that had, in Eric's words, "a 100-year history of talking to moms," it was time for radical change.

Jill: Eric, this conversation will be about Saatchi & Saatchi taking a journey in the land of youth with Kodak. It's a journey we began almost four years ago. It all started with the business objective of making Kodak the brand choice for the generation that is critical to Kodak's future, Gen Y, and specifically teen girls.

Eric: The Love/Respect Axis maps out what was happening competitively in the U.S. market in 1999. We had Polaroid with their i-Zone instant photo stickers. This was a novelty technology and very appealing to teens. It was the fad of the day, with high Love but no long-term Respect. Our other competitor, Fuji, was primarily into price competition. So they belong in the low Respect, low Love quadrant. But even there they were still serious competitors. Being a Japanese company and not subject to the quarterly pressures we face, they were able to take a long-term, 30-year-plus view of the market. On top of that, Fuji had a multi-billion-dollar war chest they could tap into to ensure their price competitiveness.

Which brings us to Kodak. You can see that for one-time-use cameras, which is the product line we are looking at, I have put us in the top left quadrant. And you can see that we were getting much stronger Love from adults than teens.

Jill: That's Kodak in 1999. How would the Love/Respect Axis look today for you with the Gen Y teen market?

Eric: I'd say we are a developing Lovemark. Not at the sweet spot yet, but well on the way. Fuji went into the market but stayed with price, and so hasn't really moved on the Axis. Polaroid never got out of the fad quadrant.

Jill: Could you outline how we worked together to capture the teen market?

Eric: As a brand for teens you have to be fun and you have to be cool. In 1999 we were doing quite well, but when you looked at the larger category, you quickly realized that everybody else was also into fun and cool.

So we analyzed both the brand and the consumers closely. We found out that relative to the category we had a heritage with some golden nuggets.

Kodak's equities are emotion, optimism, quality, and trust. All very important to teens.

So we translated them for teens to drive off of: connection, hopefulness, authenticity, and honesty. We also found that we were already part of the teen cultural vernacular. You'll have heard it: "Excuse me, can I have my Kodak moment back?" Now that's a strong, rich, deep connection.

We knew too that teens go through some very dramatic changes. Trying on different value systems, different sets of friends, different sets of clothes. Trying to figure out who they are, where they fit in, and what role they have.

We also learned that everybody wants to be around a kid with a camera.

When you have the camera in your hand, you're in control. It helps you overcome some social inhibitions. We were onto some deep, deep teen truths.

Jill: Can we look at how Mystery, Sensuality, and Intimacy helped shift Kodak to becoming a Teen Lovemark?

Eric: Let's talk first about Intimacy. Once you get below the hard surface, most teenagers are fragile individuals trying to figure out who they are and where they fit in. Our advertising created a sense of optimism and hopefulness in their quest for self-identity.

As for Mystery, just about all our TV spots show a situation that immediately intrigues kids about what's going on.

We show stories versus telling them and selling them. Let them figure things out for themselves.

Jill: A great example was the goth spot.

Eric: Sure. The spot Saatchi & Saatchi developed for us showed a goth teen taking pictures and making a collage for a school photo project. And as she makes this collage she also connects with a goth guy in her class who is another outsider. When she displays her collage, the entire class recoils in disbelief. But one boy leans forward. It's the other goth, and they smile at each other.

Jill: Where do we need to focus if Kodak is to continue to push north to the top right-hand corner of the Lovemark quadrant?

Eric: I think it's Intimacy. What sets us apart from everybody else is we can relate to the teen world.

We discovered what we call passion points—everything from music, fashion, sports, and celebrities, to entertainment and technology.

And we identified music as a teen's most important passion point.

We worked with a record company out in L.A. and found an up-and-coming boy band called Youngstown. We didn't want an established group because teens want to be part of the discovery and make a band.

Jill: Mystery, right?

Eric: Right. So we trained Youngstown to be brand stewards, and put them on a tour of 22 markets throughout the U.S. in partnership with Volunteers of America. We were in malls because this is where everything in America happens.

We did a lot of pre-event awareness-building activities—advertising, radio, Channel 1 in schools, a partnership with Sam Goody where they sold a special Youngstown pack with a one-time-use camera, a CD specific to the event, a Youngstown keychain.

Usually, events like this get maybe a couple of hundred people, but our band was drawing up to 3,000 teens per event. As the show opened there was a big Kodak splat logo, which we had designed for younger consumers, on the back of the stage.

The boys came out with their one-time-use cameras, snapping pictures of the audience. Then they'd throw the cameras out to them. It was just this massive photography love-fest.

Jill: We also developed those cool little carry cases with the Kodak logo. Kodak Wraps.

Eric: Playing to the theme of Intimacy as well. Teen girls worked on designing their dream accessory for a one-time-use camera. Designs and color choices were put up on Alloy.com, and teens voted on the final product line. Then we brought to market exactly what they recommended. That was a product created for teens by teens.

Jill: So Kodak's in a great place right now with teens, but we need to keep up the momentum. What can we do to ensure that Kodak doesn't become a fad like Polaroid?

Eric: We need to have an absolutely relentless focus on what's top-of-mind with teens today, because we know their habits change.

And we have to remain a beacon to teen girls across the nation, letting them know that it's really okay to be themselves.

Then, on top of that, we need products and services that anticipate teens' unmet needs and tap into their desires. To sum that up with two words, we need to continue to be authentic and relevant.

But the rewards for moving in the direction of a Lovemark are high. With, relatively speaking, limited funds we've achieved significant successes. The first share increase in our company's history for the one-time-use camera segment. The Number One, Two, and Three highest-scoring ads in the company's 100-plus year history. As well as improvements in brand preference and category usage. In fact, teen girls are now using one-time-use cameras 53 percent more frequently than at our starting point in 1999!

What happened?

Kodak

Chapter 12

DIAMONDS IN THE MINE

Lovemarks are owned by the people who love them. We have the power and we exercise this power every day when we go shopping.

People love to shop.
People want to buy.
People want to produce.
People want to sell.

This dynamic has made retail a 9-trillion-dollar industry throughout the world. The scale is extraordinary. Billions of shoppers browsing, choosing, and buying–every minute of every single day.

At the heart of this frantic and primal activity is shopping. Shopping is about the stuff we buy and consume but it also brings us hard up against a pressing reality: sustainability. How do we reconcile our needs and desires with how they affect the world? We cannot avoid the fact that resources are finite. That consumption has consequences. But most importantly, that a sustainable world is possible.

Many of us limit our thoughts about sustainability to our individual choices. Can I afford it, or not? We're stuck in the ritual of swipe, sign, and you're mine. Many others (around 2 billion people in fact) face sustaining life itself as a challenge every day.

Between these extremes there is a rising awareness that we are not on this planet as lone individuals. We are here with billions of others. How we consume is closely entwined with our responsibility to the future and to each other. We are starting to understand that unless we respect our shared future, there is no Love.

Consumers are becoming more and more attracted to where the Love is. Every Lovemark, whether it's a breakfast cereal, a shoe, a car, or a country, must both love and respect consumers and the world those consumers live in.

More and more consumers understand that they can make what they buy matter. Shopping as a form of activism. Choice as a tool. They want to do good and to feel good. They are no longer happy to buy sight unseen.

Retailers are starting to pick up on this demand. Stores with accurate knowledge and compelling stories about where products were sourced, who designed them, who made them. Packaging that is responsibly scaled, environmentally friendly, and still attractive.

Shoppers are in control. And everyone in business is paying new attention. Finally.

Every week someone comes up with a new twist on the fundamentals. The pop-up stores pioneered by fashion radicals Comme des Garcons echo the seasonal markets of the past. Deliveries from Amazon.com remind us of when groceries were brought to us by a young man on a bike. Kiosks mirror the stalls in every Asian village. Shopper magazines like *All You* from Time Warner and Wal-Mart have the same appeal as the traditional print catalog.

Such common threads are reassuring because they show this experimentation is bedded in a simple reality. Emotion.

Lovemarks are vital to anyone creating a shopping experience. The objective is to touch consumers and the questions are,

"What do they want out of the shopping experience?" and "How can we win Loyalty Beyond Reason?"

Shopping is not about a supply and demand curve based on economic theory. It's about empathy with customers. It's about the relationships. The relationships of the people who design and make products with the people who design and create environments for those products–and all for the delight and satisfaction of the people who shop.

My friend Dan Storper, of Putumayo World Music, is one of the people redefining the shopping experience. When Whole Foods Market asked him to bring music into their flagship Austin, Texas store he gave them a bus!

"I think retailers today like Whole Foods are really seeking to create a space in which the consumer can come in and wander and just experience the store. They wanted us to put up a display that would feature international culture, so we developed up a colorful bus inspired by the rural vehicles called *Chivas* in Colombia. Nicola Heindl, who does the great artwork on our CDs, included a similar bus on our *Colombia* CD cover. It looks wonderful and sells a lot of our CDs, DVDs, and travel journals.

"And one of the nice things is that Whole Foods has also asked us to help them do some live entertainment. So we're working with them to provide live international music for kids and adults in the outdoor plaza of the Austin store."

[Dan Storper, Putumayo World Music]

Shopping is...

Shopping is necessary.

We all have to shop for the basics of life. From the smallest village market to the largest Wal-Mart, these are the stores that supply the routines of our daily life.

Shopping is emotional.

Delight at a bargain. Satisfaction at filling the refrigerator. Anyone who thinks shopping is rational has spent too long in the office. Shoppers arrive at the store with hope, anticipation, excitement. The right experience, the perfectly pitched service, ensures they leave enchanted and uplifted. The wrong note triggers resentment and disappointment.

Shopping is primal.

We were all once proud hunters and gatherers. Make no mistake, shopping keeps those ancient spirits alive. We track, we stalk, we browse, we forage, we close in, we return home in triumph. What else explains the passions of collectors? The adidas Originals store in SoHo, New York knows that old-school is forever and plays classic hip hop to prove it.

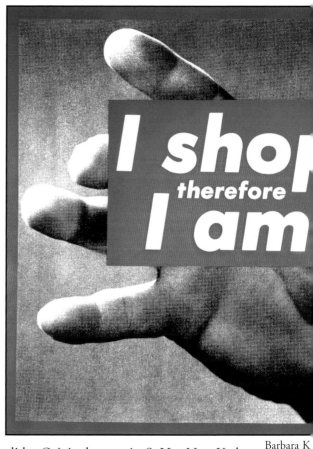

Barbara K
I shop ther

Shopping is human nature.

We surround ourselves with the things that we love. As humans we are acquisitive and curious, natural born collectors and accumulators. This is the side of us captured by stores like JACK SPADE. Great, well-designed bags and accessories as you'd expect, but also an anti-retail array of stuff that raises questions. What is it? –A ping pong paddle cover. Who is Sir Walter Scott? –Check it out on Amazon. What's with the stuffed shark? –Mystery.

Shopping is seductive.

Erma Bombeck, the voice of the American housewife in the 1960s and 1970s, once said:

"The chances of going into a store for a loaf of bread and coming out with only a loaf of bread are about 3 billion to one."

No one even bothers to go to the eclectic colette store in Paris with a list. Colette seduces in the most French way: with personality and authentic charm. Customers love just falling into their arms.

Shopping is physical.

MRI scans, lie detectors, EEG monitors, and eye motion cameras all agree. We shop with our whole body. Psychologist Dr. David Lewis discovered that while shopping during peak time in London, men's heart rates more than doubled, to 160 beats per minute. That's the same rate experienced by a fighter pilot in battle or a police officer facing a riot mob! Women's hearts don't make the same leap.

Shopping is local.

We all shop in the local, close to what is important to us, and value what makes us different. The Wegmans chain of supermarkets is grounded in the local through the extraordinary people who work there. These people give life to the shopping experience. Their mission: no customer is to leave unhappy. And no customer does.

Shopping is global.

Yes, it is a paradox. While we love what speaks to us of home, we are also drawn to what the whole world has to offer. Fresh sensory appeal. The intriguing and exciting. The signals to show we belong to global tribes, whether they're Chanel or Prada. Both have used architecture to create astonishing retail spectacle. Rem Koolhaas in New York and Herzog & de Meuron in Tokyo for Prada. Peter Marino's glass-with-class tower for Chanel in Tokyo.

Shopping is an experience.

1987

When done right, it's satisfying, pleasurable and memorable. The National Institutes of Health found that American women rate watching TV and shopping high on their list of what they find enjoyable.

Shopping is sensual.

Strolling, browsing, glancing, focusing, touching, reaching, squeezing, breathing deep, tasting, savoring. Anita Roddick knew what she was doing when she named her stores and products The Body Shop.

Shopping is fun.

Surprising, adventurous, entertaining, playful. We are curious by nature, always looking for what's new and different. We love to indulge in play. This is the world of Kitson in Los Angeles. If it's cool and hip you'll find it here–and the prices don't take themselves too seriously. This is where UGG boots live...and die.

UNITED STATES

Peter Menzel's *Material World* is a revelation. Families from around the world displaying their worldly goods. These are not images of consumers but intimate portraits of how people create their personal worlds with their possessions.

CHINA

JAPAN

KUWAIT

MONGOLIA

Shopping is social.

People do it in couples, in groups, in crowds. We take a break, have a chat, check out what is going on, engage. Apple plays to this, ensuring their staff on the floor are more like shoppers than servers: engaged, empathetic, active, and iPod-connected.

Shopping is responsible.

It's a part of the day when we are in control. Big budget or small budget, we make our choices with care and take pride in doing the best thing for our family.

Shopping matters.

Nurturing is central to family life and shopping plays an essential role. What parent doesn't try to balance what the kids want with what they believe is best for them through their shopping choices?

Shopping shapes us.

When we shop we create our identity. The cart we take to the checkout holds a portrait of our desires and needs.

Shopping is life.

Want to celebrate with friends? Go to the store first. Need to look great for a night out? Go shopping. Shopping is how we set the rhythm and feel the pulse of life. Push your way through the crowds on Saturday at Dean & Deluca in New York and you feel more alive. That's what the amazing sensuality of food can do to you. The experience is irresistible.

Shopping is winning.

In the store is where it happens. It's the place where marketers win or lose. Clothes, food, cosmetics, cars, toys. They are all subject to the same fast, direct, and tough process known as shopping. Winning the shopping challenge will be an obsession of 21st-century business.

The story of a shopper

The first time I went shopping on my own

was to the corner store on Bowerham Road in Lancaster to buy the *Lancaster Guardian* for my Dad. I was five years old.

Far better than the stack of newspapers though, were the love-hearts and pear drops and pineapple chunks displayed in huge, polished glass jars on the counter.

To this day I can smell that shop. Although most of the stock was everyday products like soap and flour, the place radiated mystery. The lighting was dim. The sensory appeal was intense.

Today's regulated retail environments pale by comparison.

Butchers used to slice into fresh meat before your eyes. The fishmonger was awash in salty water and shiny scales. The bakery produced bread, Eccles cakes, and parkin, a sort of gingerbread. Many of the dried goods were still loose in open containers as they had been for centuries.

Lancaster had not yet made the journey from trademarks to brands.

These stores were local to the core. Local stores for local people. As you would expect, everyone knew everyone. The corner shop was the center for banter and gossip. Who was visiting, who was redecorating, what was on TV last night, and the chances of the local team in the game on Saturday.

But there was a downside to this coziness. Choice was limited, and once something sold out it often took days for new stock to arrive. Service was slow and opening hours erratic. The quality was variable, prices high, and many goods definitely past their use-by date.

Today we talk about the consumer being in control. The women who did the shopping when I was a child certainly weren't. It took the retail revolution that started in the 1960s to change all that. Competition vastly improved distribution and ruthless efficiencies transformed quality and price and swept away many of the small stores.

I must have been 15 or so when the future of shopping burst into our lives. Our first local supermarket opened. What a revelation! The brand world meeting the world of the brown paper bag head-on. The modern age had arrived in Lancaster.

Shopping for dreams

My real shopper education began when I talked my way into a job with Mary Quant.

At that time she had two stores in London: the famous King's Road boutique and a more up-market version in Knightsbridge. Mary thought like a consumer. The shops, her clothes, her ranges of makeup were perfectly attuned to the times. Everything seemed effortless.

Mary believed that the role of shopping was to imagine and experiment–to dream you were more stylish and lovely, more intriguing and sensual. On her counters were lots and lots of testers to play with. A look, an attitude, a provocation. The packaging was irresistible. Very pop art, totally of the time.

As the new guy I had to learn how to apply makeup to women. My final challenge was to stand up in Selfridges department store and make up a willing member of the public. It's about the most intimate you can get with a shopper, touching her face–and there was no pity for the demonstrator who didn't get it right.

At the skin-face you learn fast that consumers have high standards and even higher expectations. Service is an art, not a science, it comes from the heart. I learned a great truth.

We weren't selling makeup at all; we were selling dreams.

The magic
of the bazaar

Where there are people there are markets.
People exchanging goods, ideas, news.
Think of the great markets of the world.
Fez, Istanbul, Tashkent, Shanghai. Names
still full of Mystery, Sensuality, and Intimacy.

When I worked in the Middle East, Rowena
and I were bazaar shoppers—frankly, there
weren't many options—and we loved it.
Bazaars offer a rich and exciting shopping
experience, like no other on earth. Modern
stores have a lot to learn from them.

Pungent smells. Calls to attract attention.
The staccato exchange of bartering. The
visual richness and the pressing of flesh.

You shop with your whole
body.

There was a wonderful store on our street in
Oasis, Casablanca, surprisingly like the
Lancaster corner stores of my childhood. It
was owned by a Moroccan of indeterminate
age who was never seen without his red fez.

Open sacks filling the air with the fragrance
of spices. Service way beyond personal; you
were an honored guest. A cacophony of
noise. The only place with a phone. This was
the store as a hub for gossip and advice.
Somehow, within this communal free-for-all,
your list was consulted, your wishes
anticipated, and your purchases attended to.

The essence of markets is bargaining. The rules are subtle. You can forget barcodes. Traipsing from seller to seller lowering the price in small increments is exciting but at the cost of the best part of a morning. The reward, however, is a hugely memorable experience.

For most of us bargaining was a lost art, but that has changed now with eBay. My youngest son, Dan, and 150 million eager users can't be wrong. People still thrill to the chase. The joy of choosing, bargaining, winning, and then enjoying.

What went wrong with supermarkets?

Somewhere in the 1990s, that great invention of the 20th century–the supermarket–reached a tipping point. Scale and standardization had already delivered unimagined efficiencies, but the pace stepped up. Consolidation through mergers and acquisitions became the new mantra. The age of hyper-competition was unleashed.

Obsessed with range and speed, novelty and functionality, and always price, price, price, supermarkets marched straight into the commodification trap.

Remember the **er** words.

Bigg**er**

Few**er**

Bet**ter**

Fast**er**

Strong**er**

Cheap**er**

Well, now you can add **Super.**

Every supermarket looks the same. Close your eyes and then open them. Are you in Beijing or Bogota?

How would you know?

All supermarkets claim "everyday low prices." All of them are lit to "search-and-destroy" mission standards. All of them treat shoppers like cattle in the aisles and sheep at the checkout. And they all play the 1980s mainstream happy music that drives you crazy.

Everybody's doing the same research. Everybody's got the same shelf-management system. Everybody's working with the same financial model.

It's an endgame. The shopping experience is one of the great missed opportunities. The moment when shoppers become buyers. The moment when inspired personal service can transform "might think about" into "must have."

Consumers make up to 80 percent of their decisions about what to buy while they are in the supermarket, and yet ways to help them choose have hardly advanced for decades.

> "Humans now have to make more decisions in a single day than a caveman did in a lifetime."
>
> [Dr. Aric Sigman, *The Explosion of Choice: Tyranny or Freedom*]

In one supermarket, psychologist Dr. Aric Sigman counted 83 different shampoos, 68 shower gels, 42 deodorants, 77 washing powders, and 87 breakfast cereals.

Lovemarks explain exactly what's gone wrong. Supermarkets went for Respect at the price of Love.

As shoppers we gained quality, selection, and price, but we lost so much from the experience. Worse still, we can't tell one store from another, and most of us don't care.

Can aircraft hangar-sized stores really become Lovemarks? Sure they can. Can the 24/7 hustle of the convenience store win Loyalty Beyond Reason? Why not. Do Lovemarks point the way for all stores to create long-term relationships with shoppers? Count on it.

The Theater of Dreams

The drama of Lovemarks can be brought to life in the store. They can transform the shopping environment into a Theater of Dreams and the shopping experience into a delight.

The evocative name, Theater of Dreams, comes from one of the most emotional, most inspiring of human activities: sport.

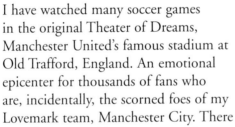

I have watched many soccer games in the original Theater of Dreams, Manchester United's famous stadium at Old Trafford, England. An emotional epicenter for thousands of fans who are, incidentally, the scorned foes of my Lovemark team, Manchester City. There is nothing quite like being part of a crowd, humming with anticipation, leaping to celebrate a goal, and sharing great stories of victory or defeat.

That's the experience I want when I shop as well. Shopping is being reinvented right now by creative and passionate people. People who are confident in their judgment and taste. Who think they know best—and are proud of it!

Curators like Murray Moss whose store in lower Manhattan is gallery-like and sophisticated. The thread that draws a shopper along the large glass cases item by item is the taste of Murray Moss. Since 1994, Moss's sensibility has connected the perfect Bocca sofa with the perfect Aliseo champagne flute, Massimo Giacon's Pigface pencil sharpener with Marc Berthier's Tykho radio. This is a store with precision and integrity as well as an inspiring sense of purpose: to help amazing objects capture shoppers in five seconds. And the staff on the floor extend the gallery metaphor. They have that wonderful combination of expertise lovingly combined with boundless enthusiasm.

Provocateurs like Tristan Eaton and Paul Budnitz of Kid Robot in LA and SoHo, New York are making global urban vinyl a sensation. Stores for the curious as well as hard-core fans. Crowded, busy, and dedicated. Here, the release of a super-limited edition figure of Dumb Luck Rabbit is a cause for jubilation. Dumb Luck? I don't think so.

Talent scouts like Remo Giuffré, who created my favorite online store, REMO General Store, in Australia. REMO prides itself on quality and passion, a community of shoppers, and an eclectic range of products. My favorite? A swim cap with a red fez on it! Perfect for a Turkish bath.

"When I was a teenager I loved their eclectic catalogs full of great T-shirts and amazing things from around Australia and around the world. REMO isn't just a store, it's a community of folks who love the interesting and useful. Customer suggestions and ideas drive the product range. Retailing with a dash of serendipity. Extraordinary things, now international, thanks to the Internet."

[Lovemarks.com nomination by Joy, Australia]

Purists like the founders of MUJI, the Japanese no-brand. MUJI bath products, MUJI stationery, MUJI slippers, MUJI bicycles, MUJI furniture, and now–the MUJI house. Understated packaging, a passion for sustainability, and the determination to change the world.

Conjurers like architect Jon Jerde, who made real urban retail fantasies like Langham Place in Kowloon and the Lakefront Complex in the Bellagio in Las Vegas.

Retail is buzzing.

And the buzz is now resonating in the everyday world of the supermarket. Smart retailers are exploring the big, wide world of shopping and putting their insights to work in the supermarket.

How? They are looking at the traditional supermarket format through the eyes of the shopper.

The supermarket

Knows shoppers spend an average of 21 minutes a visit

Packs the store with over 50,000 differently branded items

Works on the More Means More principle, squeezing as many items on each shelf as possible

Is mesmerized by incremental changes to products

Believes the bigger the shopping cart, the bigger the purchases

Thinks kids plus shopping is a "slow-down" problem

Has staff trained to answer questions

Uses checkout time as a chance to pitch advertising

Provides well-lit car parks (if you're lucky)

Knows to three decimal points the number of car parks per square foot of selling space

Believes taste tests are the pinnacle of shopper interaction

Feels under pressure from suppliers, regulators, consumers, competitors

The shopper...

Feels every shopping experience is unique

Finds shopping for what she needs like looking for a needle in a haystack

Can only buy from what she sees—and sees less than half of what's on the shelf

Flashes through a category in a mere 1.4 seconds

Wishes they'd put the art back into cart and design one that won't give her a hernia

Loves the kids to have fun, wherever they are. A magician in a supermarket. A clown. Bring 'em on!

Wonders why no one ever offers to help

Dreams of checking out as she shops, not when she's finished

Would feel more loved if they threw in a free car wash

Just wants to park closer to the door

Is bored by samples-on-a-stick. She knows there are more entertaining ways to tempt her to taste

Feels confused, tired, and frustrated. Can't wait to get in and out

The store is the ultimate arena for great ideas to play and make a real difference. Here products are exposed to the desires of shoppers. What she doesn't notice in 60 days is gone in 90 days. Sensuality is the fast-track. The ability to engage on a primal level of scent, motion, touch, taste, and whispers. The triggers that arouse us to what is important. We are, after all, choosing what we will eat, wear next to our skin, drive in, and play with.

People want to sip the tea, taste the cheese, stroke the diaper, sniff the shampoo, and weigh the pack in their hand. Sampling as a special event is history. People want to interact with anything they buy if they choose to, not just products on promotion.

All stores pay lip service to the idea of service. But few of them understand that service is about empathy–not command and control.

When I am looking for something, I want guidance, not direction. A perfect example is the way I am treated at a local specialist chocolate shop, Vosges Haut. No barrage of "you must try this," "we recommend that" here. It is as if the staff behind the counter are tuned into my radar. One of them noticed and commented on my black shirt, a favorite purchased in France. From there we moved to a joint love of sport. Was I in a mood to stay on and shop after that? You bet. And I did. After all I felt I was amongst friends. This sort of empathy is not easy, it can quickly fall into flattery. Done well, empathy is the diamond in the mine.

FORGET THE RULES

Shoppers are not alien beings. They are a gift. An inspiration for ideas and innovation. Everyone you meet is talking about "doing retail." Some start with consumers. Very few are starting with shoppers.

Today's shopper refuses to compromise.

She wants familiarity and she demands variety.
She wants the fastest route to the checkout and to have fun in her few spare minutes.
She wants great food and won't spend much time making it.
She wants cereal shelved with fruit and dairy and organics.
She wants to purchase on impulse and insists on value.
She wants a beautifully wrapped package and the option of "Paper or plastic?"
She wants efficient service and empathy with her moods.

She is willing to be Loyal Beyond Reason to her Lovemarks store.

How to get started? Study how great businesses don't just break the rules, they transform them.

You have to have a key to start a car. *Tell it to Prius*

You can't let people on airlines eat their meals when they feel like it. That's anarchy. *Tell it to Virgin Airlines*

Airlines don't do retail. *Tell it to Song*

Shoppers like to know the exact price they are paying before they purchase. *Tell that to eBay*

No one is ever going to pay $3 for a cup of coffee. Even in New York City. *Someone forgot to tell Starbucks*

Shoppers are easily overwhelmed by choice. *Tell that to Amazon.com*

Only kids play games. *Tell that to the Grand Theft Auto Franchise*

The great retailers understand that their business is connecting consumers to brands and then to Lovemarks.

That's why 7-Eleven, dismissed for years as a chain of dingy convenience stores, is now among the most innovative merchandisers in America. How? A change in ownership and a change in attitude. Simply put, 7-Eleven now puts consumers first. Predicting what 7-Eleven's consumers want has become an obsession. The eyes and ears of its stores have become a serious competitive advantage.

All convenience stores sell the same thing. *Tell it to 7-Eleven!!*

The future of supermarkets–Sunka

When most people talk about the future of the supermarket, they talk technology. Wireless neon signs, infra-red signals, handheld scanners, smart shopping carts, radio frequency identification.

All fantastic innovations, but they are not the future. One by one they will become tablestakes just as freezers and barcodes and conveyor belts did before them.

The only way to spring the commodity trap is with Mystery, Sensuality, and Intimacy.

I have seen this future and it is called La Sala Sunka, an inspired concept springing out of Lleida, near Barcelona in Spain.

The Pujol family's chain of neighborhood food stores didn't panic when the powerful hypermarket formula started to bite. Instead they created Sunka.

The Pujol's research said "demanding and stressed people" made up 33 percent of consumers, mostly couples with kids who were under pressure at work and at home. Sunka was created for them.

Not a specialty store, but a store focused on special shoppers.

In defiance of all the rules, Sunka's first spaces don't sell, but introduce a deceleration zone. To wind back the stress levels, the work of local young artists is hung, framed by haiku and insights.

Then the concierge. Leave your clothes to be cleaned, shoes to be mended, photographs to be developed. There's a fax, access to the Internet, a photocopier. Solutions for everyday frustrations like home repairs and day care.

Fresh fruit comes first, with wonderful fragrances and colors. Aromatherapy! Then flavor therapy in the prepared meals. Forget the usual convenience meals where it's the convenience of distributors and retailers that counts and enjoy the next evolutionary step: food kits.

Think TV dinner–and then forget it. Yes, the complete meal is here but it's not processed beyond recognition. These kits include all the fresh ingredients for a proper meal. Recipe included. And if you want the fish steamed–no problem. Free of charge and done to perfection.

The prices are in line with any other supermarket with the message: forget about price. <u>Our</u> job is to match our competitors. <u>Your</u> job is to enjoy shopping.

And once you're done, get it delivered. You've got until 11PM–this is Spain after all.

Thanks to Lluis Martinez-Ribes from the ESADE Business School in Barcelona for opening the door to Sunka.

The transformation of shopping

Every store, every stall, every kiosk, every website needs to aspire to become a Lovemark to the shoppers it serves. Lovemarks create what I call right-side-up shopping, where retailers face shoppers rather than their own processes and problems.

The big price and efficiency gains have already been made. Incremental improvements remain, but they'll not be enough to differentiate. Worse still, winning the price wars has been at a cost for some retailers. Their reputation. Wal-Mart is an obvious example. Still admired and respected by shoppers, imagine the possibilities if Wal-Mart were loved!

With Lovemarks, shopping can be transformed by shoppers.

Shoppers who want to know where products came from and how they were made. Shoppers who make their choices with understanding and skill. Shoppers who want to enjoy the experience. Shoppers who ask questions about ingredients and packaging. Shoppers who want to deal with stores and products they respect, and may grow to love. Shoppers who care.

You want to see the future of shopping? Look at the passion in these consumer nominations sent into Lovemarks.com

amazon.com

If you love books you've got to love Amazon.com. The thrill of getting the Amazon box in the mail, the contents beautifully packed in those great squishy air bags. Amazon, a mighty river of love flowing right to my door.

[Antonio, Italy]

 THE BODY SHOP

The Body Shop has a strong attitude, but a soft tone of voice. It is a pioneer. Because it isn't just nice packaging with the same ingredients. The Body Shop has a soul and I like that soul, it is my friend.

[Gun, Turkey]

BARNES & NOBLE
BOOKSELLERS

My time at Barnes & Noble is relaxing and private! It is not a library because of the "quiet" hustle and bustle of other Barnes & Noble addicts. I always stop by the books recommended by the staff. Their descriptions of the books often intrigue me enough to purchase them. This must be my favorite place to purchase gifts! Gift cards, books, bookmarks, journals, and CDs. Have you ever been in a store, loved the music playing, and wanted to know who the artist was? At Barnes & Noble the CD playing is displayed for you to see. Love it!

[Brenda, United States]

1. Look through the eyes of the shopper. The closer you get to her experience, the richer and smarter your responses.

2. Shake up your ideas. Selling stuff is an ideas business. Spend time in stores you've never ventured into. What are their ideas? What works, what doesn't?

3. Imagine your brand in a Theater of Dreams. What makes this place different, compelling, inspiring? Now get to it and make it happen.

4. Expand your shopping horizons. Look out to the rest of the world. As human beings we've forgotten as much about shopping as we've remembered. Dig deep.

5. Examine your principles. What do you truly believe in? Is your store and your brand founded on those principles?

Five things
to do tomorrow

Chapter 13

I CAN SEE CLEARLY NOW

The parallels between the issues facing brands

I have always been curious. To be the best in anything, you have to be curious about everything and take nothing for granted. Einstein, one of the greatest minds of the last century, described himself as "neither especially clever nor especially gifted." Then he added, "I am only very, very curious."

The most curious people in business ought to be marketers. Eager to learn, fascinated by the strange passions of human beings, always asking questions, always in pursuit of the strange, the unusual, or the simply interesting. Most marketers, and to my regret many researchers, are not like this at all.

I am a passionate advocate for anyone who sets out to explore, to discover, and to innovate.

Why has the enterprise of research turned from passionate enquiry to an obsession with detail? When exactly did metric mania take over? When did researchers stop being the people who ask the best questions, the people who know the weird stuff? When I look around I see a profession that has lost itself in a cul-de-sac of testing, evaluation, measurement, and risk management.

Most businesses working in the same field have access to the same market information as their competitors. They all research the same stuff using the same processes and–not surprisingly–get the same numbers. But looking at the numbers is not where the game is going to be won. This is where curiosity counts. The very human quality of wanting-to-know–that's what I believe can transform research and put it back where it belongs: at the heart of the action and making emotional connections with consumers. It's time to get some rock 'n' roll into research! Open up, kick back, and dream. To transform brands into Lovemarks, we need to transform research.

nd the issues facing research are hard to ignore.

Research (like brands) has developed into a multi-billion-dollar global industry. ESOMAR (World Association of Opinion and Marketing Research Professionals, for those of you who don't belong) estimates that the research industry has revenues of $15 billion worldwide.

Like research, brands have become satisfied with incremental improvement. It is hard not to think of the two of them without seeing them tied together. The new challenge was perfectly described in a discussion with Malcolm Gladwell, author of *The Tipping Point*.

"The allegiance that people have to certain brands is not always knowable or quantifiable, and it might be sometimes a mistake to try and ascertain what the nature of that X is. We don't really know why we have it, and you can't figure it out. We simply have it."

Just as Lovemarks offer a new path for brands, so too can Lovemarks inform a new path for research. A path that can lead to far deeper connections with consumers through Mystery, Sensuality, and Intimacy. And this path leads us straight to the power and value of insights.

We need research to help us discover what we don't know we don't know. To find bigger problems to solve. And then we need research to inspire us to go further and deeper. We need to face a bunch of issues we have avoided so far. How to deal with the rich variety of experience? How to factor in the senses when they use such fine-grained distinctions? How to touch what is bubbling below the surface of consciousness?

We have to look at people's lives in their entirety, the things they hope for and dream about, the things they fear, the things they love, the things they hate and need and want. What bores them. We need to understand what has meaning and significance for them, not just what they buy and use.

Malcolm Gladwell again:

"I am interested in what it means to take the unconscious seriously in marketing and other realms. Much of psychology at the moment is consumed with taking the unconscious seriously after a gap of 50 years. But it is a return in a much more sophisticated way than previously, exploring the role the unconscious plays in decision making, in impression formation, preference formation.

"Once you take the unconscious seriously you undermine virtually all quantitative market research and its focus. This is very good news for the creative part of the advertising world, and bad news for the number-crunchers.

"Inside the heart of every marketer beats a control fanatic. They want a quantifiable process, and they would like to introduce a level of transparency to things that are necessarily oblique.

"In my new book, I am interested by this question: When you ask someone how they feel, how seriously can you take their answer? And the answer to that is, not very seriously. And yet the temptation to take their answer at face value is nearly overwhelming in all domains, not just marketing."

Lovemarks need research, but a different kind of research. I know that I am rarely asked my opinion as a consumer. I presume my transactions are data-tracked and batch-analyzed by computer, but I never get asked for my stories. We need research that puts consumers at the center rather than at the base of a very large pyramid. And I'm not talking about just turning the PowerPoint upside-down!

I'm looking for research that counts the beats of your heart rather than the fingers of your hand. Research that connects with the inner life of the consumer. Not as statistical constructs. Not as they were. Not as you would like them to be, but as they truly are: living, feeling beings full of fears and desires, hopes and dreams. Kris Kristofferson got it: "A walkin' contradiction/Partly truth and partly fiction."

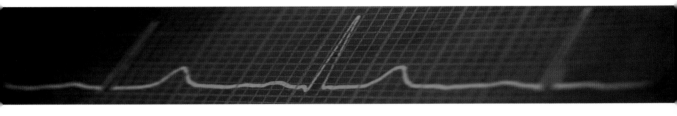

Fresh and true insights are the way into the inner life of the consumer. Peter Cooper of the London research company QualiQuant International offered us this one:

"The way people personalize computers or other ordinary, everyday objects around the home is a very significant way in which people make sense out of the world. One of the earliest studies I was involved in was for Electrolux, the appliance manufacturer. I was always struck by a remark from one particular housewife up in Manchester, England. She described her spin dryer like this, 'My spin dryer to me is called Fred, and I have a relationship with Fred which is often better than the one I have with my husband.'"

As Lovemarks take onboard the best attributes of brands, so the new research will be created out of the best techniques of current research.

The failure of research to truly engage with consumers is not just a problem for researchers. It's a problem most people in any business share.

I discovered this first-hand when I was working in the Middle East for Procter & Gamble. Like other companies at the time, P&G's research was done by the numbers. Sometimes it seemed to me that we did little other than to verify what we already knew. We were tied to benchmarks and followed norms. I found it tough to see the value of all this, so I spent as much time as I could out of the office, three weeks out of four.

My passion was store checks and home visits. After going through all the numbers, I'd head into Dubai and visit a hundred little shops in the Soukh and get myself invited into consumers' homes. I talked with retailers, consumers, people just walking by. Irrespective of what the share numbers said, I got my insights from these connections.

When the store visits indicated the trends, I knew whether I had the right distribution model, the right pricing model, and the right packaging lineup. My conversations with store owners and what I saw with my own eyes told me if our fundamentals were on track.

Once I'd done the store checks, I'd go into homes and watch the women at work. I'd sit down with a woman and watch her life and the lives of her kids. I'd get an understanding of how much time she spent with her husband, how he dressed, what he dressed in, where he went, and what people's reactions were. I learned what mattered to them as a family.

As I got to know some of these women, they'd let me look into their laundry baskets, allow me to check out their cupboards. Some of these people were very poor. Some didn't even have underclothes. The lesson was obvious. While we had been very concerned in our advertising with helping our consumers wash fine fabrics, guess what? Most of them didn't have any!

I learned that unless you get to know people and stand beside them as they work, you will find out only what they believe you want to know.

I found this to be true time and time again. When I was working for Pepsi, I found one of my local cafes would buy private-label cola and pour it into their one Pepsi bottle. When a customer turned up they would always be served a "Pepsi." You could interrogate the numbers till you're blue in the face and never get close to that insight into how people truly valued the brand.

To undertake Lovemarks research wherever you are means developing close relationships with consumers. In the Middle East this could mean markets and cafes. In the United States we could be talking sports games and schoolyards.

Without a doubt many consumers are highly informed and deeply suspicious of marketing. What they do respond to, however, is passion. No one can resist enthusiasm. If you are searching for insight because you love your product, the results can be extraordinary.

At Saatchi & Saatchi we group our research into three approaches. I believe these approaches can transform the way businesses connect with consumers:

1. Climb a mountain

2. Go to the jungle

3. Think like a fish

If you want to look at a tree, stay on the ground. If you want to see the forest, climb a mountain.

There is no doubt about it. Lovemarks build from the ground up. One person at a time. Now, connecting with people one-on-one is very powerful, but people as a rule don't live in isolation. Hermits are rare. People love to be together. As members of teams, clubs, and organizations, of families, couples, and communities. You name it, people like to do most things with someone else.

This means that we have to see the big picture to make meaningful connections with individual consumers. Yes, it's a paradox. How to inspire people as part of the groups that matter to them, and do it with the intimate finesse that distinguishes a Lovemark.

Like all great paradoxes there is no simple resolution, but you can take a fantastic point of view. The view from the peaks.

I have always had an uneasy relationship with stat flacks. My gut instinct is to protect intuition from measurement. To nurture ideas away from the glare of metrics. To feel about, rather than factor in.

But I also know that when 100,000 people act on their own emotional needs, you had better have some idea of the direction they might turn in. And you probably don't have enough time to knock on each door!

I made just this point at a conference run by ESOMAR. I challenged the pros to make consumer emotion their priority. I told them it made no sense to measure emotion according to traditional scales. That they needed to invent some measures that do make sense.

I also promised I would come back to one of their conferences once they had worked out how to count the beats of their hearts, not the fingers of their hands.

The challenge was taken up by Peter Cooper of QualiQuant International. Peter is also passionate about measuring emotion in a responsive and smart way. He knew there had to be something after brands, and he immediately saw Lovemarks as a possible framework for taking the next step. And he was convinced that the Love/Respect Axis offered a new way to articulate emotion very precisely.

"When you take the Lovemarks quadrant of the Axis, I can see there are different types of Love which will give more or less weight to Respect. For example, you have a parental form of relationship where the consumer will be leaning very heavily upon

certain brands because they are more on the Respect side. Then you have more romantic types of relationships where people talk passionately, particularly about the sensory aspects or feelings that they have about certain brands."

QualiQuant teamed up with Saatchi & Saatchi for some intensive testing of Lovemarks. What did I love about their approach? They saw the qualitative and the quantitative as a tight unit. Heart and hand, together.

Peter and his colleague John Pawle created a set of sophisticated questions to measure emotion.

The results of the first tests from QualiQuant? They exceeded everything we had hoped for.

For a start, they demonstrated beyond a doubt that consumers do feel passionately about some special brands. Better still, they showed that people feel just the way that Lovemarks predicted. And they showed that Love and Respect are what matter. The correlation between the two is 0.60, if that's the way your mind works.

From this understanding of consumers comes our remarkable evidence that Lovemarks do have huge commercial benefits—in terms of preference, in terms of usage, in terms of future purchase. If you can move your brand into the Lovemark

quadrant, it's lifelong relationships, lifetime loyalty, and premium profits.

As the great mountain climber Sir Edmund Hillary said when he stood on the peak of Mt. Everest: "We knocked the bugger off!"

Lovemarks can guide strategy, positioning, creative, and tracking, and they can do it across every touchpoint.

At Saatchi & Saatchi, we had known in our hearts that our intuitions about Lovemarks were rock solid. Now we have the figures to back it up.

Lovemarks not only claim a place in the hearts of consumers, they can stand up and be counted.

2. Go to the jungle

Xploring is based on a very simple principle.

If you want to understand how a lion hunts, don't go to the zoo, go to the jungle.

Xploring came out of our attempts to understand China. 1.3 billion people, 3.7 million square miles, and 40 new babies every minute! At Saatchi & Saatchi, we believe that Nothing is Impossible.

We began by encouraging our clients to invest in better, more insightful research. We invested our own money and time in focus groups and discussions, fact-finding and analysis. Essentially, we gathered a lot of information.

Most businesses gather information about consumers by going to the zoo. They put respondents in a "viewing" room, feed them snacks, and let them go through the motions of responding to questions with a "trained" moderator. Someone who can lead them, direct them…maybe even control them.

While focus groups can have a place, they are deeply flawed. They certainly didn't give us rich insights into the Chinese as a people. What they taught us was about the Chinese consumer not as a person…but as a respondent. By bringing them into our environment, asking them our questions, and using our moderator, we were simply gathering information—and we wanted more.

Enter Xploring. It is probably the oldest research technique ever used. But despite its effectiveness, most companies seem to have forgotten about it.

Ironically, Xploring is far easier to conduct, more affordable, and far more insightful and inspiring than traditional research.

Simply put, the Xplorer puts on a pair of comfortable shoes, grabs a backpack, and heads off.

There are no one-way viewing mirrors. No projective techniques. Just interaction, observation, and lots of conversation.

We've been invited into countless homes, hung out with kids in video arcades, gone to work with women, exercised with school children, dug through people's fridges, drunk beer with men, cooked dinner with families, had tea with teenagers, worked out with moms, changed diapers, rode roller coasters, cleaned bathrooms, sung karaoke, cried over broken marriages, screamed over football.

Saatchi & Saatchi's seven-person research team in China has now travelled over 25,000 miles throughout the country, most of it by van, some by boat, some by train. That's the equivalent of circling the planet!

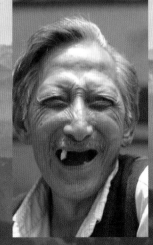

In those travels we have met 22-year-old millionaires, and gas station attendants with dreams to own their own business.

We have met children whose ambition is to learn English, not so they can study abroad, but so they can make China stronger in the world market.

Children with ambitions to keep China clean. Old men who believe today's China is a woman's world. And young students who believe the future of the world's economy is firmly in the hands of China.

To be successful in China, we have to stop being lured blindly by the sheer scale of the market (and it is amazing) and take the time to understand its people—and most importantly, what motivates them. As A.G. Lafley of P&G says, "Answers aren't just found in numbers. You have to get out and look."

By doing just that, we came away from our first Xploring trip with insights that I don't believe we could have arrived at any other way.

| The Chinese people have a deep sense of humor that encompasses both slapstick and sophisticated plays on language.

|| The women of China have achieved a high measure of financial equality. Now they are struggling for recognition and higher status.

||| Like people everywhere, what the Chinese say is not necessarily how they feel, but the fear of loss of face adds a new layer of complexity.

|||| The Chinese are in Love with romance. It is not the past that the Chinese today respond to.

𝍢 They are motivated by their passion to make China great in the future.

𝍢 | There are no VCRs. There are many DVDs. China is not slowed by decades of technological baggage, and leaps straight to the best new offerings.

𝍢 || Consumers in China don't fear technology. They crave it.

𝍢 ||| The Chinese do not want to become Western. What they do want is to gain respect for being Chinese. Western icons and imagery interest them. Respect for what is Chinese connects with them.

It is not difficult to see how emotional connections can be inspired by any of these insights. And the beauty of Xploring is that it can be easily conducted on a supermarket floor, in a busy city street, in a kitchen, or anywhere else that consumers live their lives. The key ingredients are the passion and the curiosity of the Xplorers.

P&G have taken the "go to the jungle" idea and developed it as an approach they expect from everyone in the company. Jim Stengel, P&G's Global Marketing Officer, puts it like this:

"What P&G tries to do is to be very closely and personally in touch with our consumers. This means being out there with them and participating in the ways they live their lives. And that's not just calling them or sending them an Internet survey. It's about being in their homes, shopping with them, watching them as they use our products, talking to them about their lives. For senior people, junior people, everybody at P&G, our culture means being a part of our Consumer's life."

Jim reveals a host of insights discovered at the consumer's side. Insights that have not only shaped how P&G talks with consumers, but also how they have developed new products. Here's one example of how effective this kind of research can be:

"In the United States we sell a lot of Tide in outlets where they sell very large sizes of products at a discount. In the end we came to the point where we were making the detergent bottles so big and heavy that our consumers were having trouble lifting them! But, because we saw the problem in action in the supermarkets and at home, we knew we needed to act. Our solution was to put a spout on the bottom of the bottle, like a beer tap. This meant that whoever was doing the washing could push a little button and hold a cup underneath the bottle to get the amount of Tide they wanted for the wash.

"You don't get an idea like that by sitting in a room. It happened when we were watching consumers struggling to pour out of very big bottles of detergent in their own laundries at home."

The reverse situation came out of the same sort of observation in the Middle East. There, P&G people noticed that women often could not afford a box of Ariel for their washing. So they began selling Ariel in small sachets. Now households could spread the cost of washing and still avoid going down to the river with a bar of hard soap.

Masao Inoue, the Chief Engineer of Toyota's fuel-efficient vehicle, the Prius, ventured out to do his own Xploring. He was working on a new model for the very different American market.

"Baseball is very popular in Los Angeles, so I went and watched a game there. I parked my Prius in the parking lot and then watched the game. When I walked back to the parking lot I found my car was surrounded by larger cars and pick-up trucks. The Prius looked very, very small against them. I just felt it very strongly. It is something that you have to experience, to feel. So my thought was that the Prius as it was might be too small for the United States market. By being there and seeing the different sizes I learned something you can't really learn from reading the size and measurements of the car.

3. Think like a fish

The Māori of Aotearoa, New Zealand, say: "If you want to catch a fish, first learn to think like a fish."

Working with consumers and learning to think and feel as they do is how Lovemarks happen.

We have already seen how powerful it can be to go out and join consumers where they live. To participate, not just observe. Another successful idea is to work with consumers to develop insights. I am not talking focus groups here, but interactive sessions where consumers can make a specific difference to design, service, production, distribution.

When Nike decided to develop a store concept designed for women, they knew that they would need a lot of help from women themselves. Clare Hamill of Nike discusses exactly how much:

"When we decided to create the Goddess stores, we knew we wanted a real one-on-one client relationship. In fact, we wanted more than one-on-one—we wanted a situation where we would be listening and interacting. So if somebody's actually saying 'Hey, I'm not going to buy this, it doesn't work for me,' we'll work to get that feedback back into our products and product teams."

Clare and her people at the Nike Goddess stores talked with consumers about time and balance, the complexities of their lives and shopping, as well as what moves them to participate in sports and fitness activities. Taking customer suggestions and ideas seriously is fundamental to creating Lovemarks. But at Nike Goddess they took another step forward.

"The only way to make a product that is loved is to have the people who use it involved in the process of making it. We certainly use our athletes for this. Michael Jordan works with our designers, and at Nike Goddess we have groups of women that we bring in and work with. We know that we have to find the woman we are selling to. To find her and work with her. One of the women we worked with in this way was Max. She worked with the product teams. It's such a great idea for product teams to have a face and a name and an inspiration. A consumer who really does tell them firsthand what she thinks."

P&G believes in the value of consumer ideas so much that they have built a special facility to ensure the interaction is as dynamic and inspirational as possible.

About 30 miles outside Cincinnati, inside a nondescript building, P&G has designed and created a typical consumer's home and a store. Consumers are invited in to help

P&G design new products and refine others that are already on the shelves. The consumers become participants to the point of having a shower and giving the product team live feedback on the size and scent of soaps.

These examples show the prerequisite of Lovemarks research: the personal participation of consumers. And this is where the Internet is developing as an extraordinarily effective research resource. It is clear that the web is set to play an increasingly important role in adventurous and creative research.

The Internet as a medium has been bogged down by effectiveness metrics: hits and clicks rather than discovering how we can change people's lives.

My experience with consumers convinces me that there is emotional life on the Internet, and we can tap into it.

Peter Cooper of QualiQuant International is at the leading edge of computer-assisted research, on- and off-line.

"The computer screen as a research tool has many advantages. Interviewing does not have to be done on-line, and can be in a computer-assisted form as well. What we have demonstrated time and time again, in both cases, is that if you remove the interviewer from the situation, you can create a spontaneous dialogue between the respondent and the computer screen. Respondents are much more likely to freely express their emotions and to be honest about themselves. In other words, we've removed the 'critic,' which is the interviewer.

"This is not to imply that interviewers are always critics, but rather that without the interviewer, much in the same way as one might daydream, our emotions are likely to emerge in an uncensored form. We can very quickly and economically create the sort of data in a quantitative form that you would normally see in a well-run focus group.

"The method is also highly interactive. Material can be collected and fed back to the respondent almost instantaneously. We do not have to confront people with the usual segmented, differential scales which oblige them to act in a more rational way. Those sorts of scales are fine for measuring aspects of Respect, for example, but not for Love and other emotions. To measure emotion we need visual and verbal images and projective approaches, which the interplay between computer screen and respondent readily stimulates."

1. Give your brains a rest. There is nothing wrong with thinking but thinking demands action to make any sense You can't think your way into relationships, insights, great ideas. You have got to create them, have them, DO them. Love them.

2. Kick the information addiction Remember that reason and information only produce conclusions, not action That's where you need to open up to emotion

3. Embrace emotion Feel it yourself, don't just analyze it in consumers. This is how long-term relationships are made.

4. Go to the edge Everyone at the center thinks the same way. That's why they ended up there in the first place The edge is unsettled and risky. Perfect to shake up conventions and formulas and come up with new ideas.

5. Stand for your local. Great ideas come from somewhere They get and keep their juice by knowing what they stand for. Wherever you are, make it your mission to love what matters there: movies, sports, music, language.

Five things
to do tomorrow

Chapter 14

I'LL FOLLOW THE SUN

Lovemarks are owned by the people who love them. That's simple enough. But just as the consumer's point of view (rather than simply that of the brand) comes into focus, something else becomes very clear. Some people take their Love of a brand very seriously indeed.

These are the people who would be shocked by the very idea of the "passive consumer," so loved by marketing manuals and anti-brand activists. They are the ones who promote and advocate for their brand. The ones who organize for reinstatement, who suggest improvements and refinements, who create websites and spread the word. They are also the people who act as moral guardians for the brands they love. They make sure that wrongs are righted and hold the brand fast to its stated principles.

I call them Inspirational Consumers.

"When you think about viral marketing and the people who turn others on to your service and recommend it highly, they are your Inspirational Consumers. These are consumers who themselves market the things they are passionate about. So, they might say, 'Oh, haven't you flown JetBlue?' and they all but sell you the tickets and put you on the plane! For the company, they become the buzz marketing arm. In the early days of Yahoo! we had a lot of that. Now you can see it too with Google. People are just passionate about Google, and they can't help themselves from telling their friends about it. For Yahoo! our Inspirational Consumers are the ones that, without getting any marketing dollars from us, tell people about our services."

[Tim Sanders, Chief Solutions Officer, Yahoo!, and author of *Love Is the Killer App*]

In 1985, it was Inspirational Consumers who told the Coca-Cola Company in no uncertain terms that New Coke was not going to replace traditional Coca-Cola. And that was that. Too bad about the $4 million investment in market research and over 200,000 blind taste tests. It may in principle (or even in fact) have tasted better, but these Coke lovers didn't care. A deluge of phone calls and letters demanded the return of the original Coca-Cola.

A group of Inspirational Consumers formed the Society for the Preservation of the Real Thing. There was panic buying. In San Antonio, Texas, a local man drove to the town's bottler and bought $1,000 worth of "real" Coca-Cola.

And Coke got the message. It took less than three months for this huge company to respond to the consumer tide of outrage, and return to the original ingredients. Coke acknowledged that it is the consumer who owns a Lovemark, not the company.

The New Coke debacle has become legendary, but I am interested in those consumers who caused the turmoil and turnaround. Coke's website pays tribute to them today by posting New Coke memories. This one is my favorite:

"My family and I have been active Coke drinkers for my entire life. I recall a time when Coca-Cola decided to change the formula; there was havoc amongst the members of my household. I believe there was a date when the new Coke would be sold and the old Coke would be removed from the shelves. My father, who is a tremendous Coke consumer, panicked, rushed to the store, and bought several cases of what is now Coke classic. These Cokes only lasted two weeks. I was a child when this happened, and I recall my father grounding me for drinking his 'old Coke,' which he held as priceless. Thank God for the return of Coke classic or my family may still be in mayhem."

As Roger Enrico, former CEO of arch-rival Pepsi-Cola, said in his well-known book *The Other Guy Blinked*, "By the end of their nightmare, [Coca-Cola] figured out who they really are. Caretakers." He might have added…"of a Lovemark."

Those blind tests were blind alright. They forgot to ask the key question:

"How would you feel if we changed Coca-Cola to this new formula?"

That's the question that would have allowed their Inspirational Consumers to warn them of the consequences. And make it very clear to them that the line, "The best just got better" was never going to fly.

Inspirational Consumers understand that the Love of a brand goes two ways. When a consumer loves you enough to take action, any action, it is time to take notice. Immediately.

Be honest. How many suggestion cards have you left in a box waiting until you had the time to look at them? How many times have you side-stepped an irate customer because you didn't need the stress? And isn't it a little weird that you never get a single e-mail from a consumer? Ever. Yes, business protects itself well, and consumers know it. But in these consumers lie the seeds of inspiration.

So start thinking of these people who love what you do as Inspirational Consumers. Help them get behind your brand and watch it accelerate into a Lovemark.

Inspirational Consumers build fan sites, Inspirational Consumers act as the catalyst for word-of-mouth campaigns, Inspirational Consumers can make great products better, Inspirational Consumers have ideas that matter, ideas that can transform your brand—if you will let them.

In my experience, Inspirational Consumers not only love a brand, they also love people. That's what gives them their emotional drive–what gives them their sheer stamina.

They are the first voice in the game of tag we call "word-of-mouth."

What was the most famous television commercial ever produced in the history of the world?

Apple. 1984. Right? Only ran once at the Superbowl. When people first saw it that Sunday night, I don't believe anybody got it. What was she doing with that hammer? And then…word-of-mouth.

The best thing you can do is entertain and stimulate through a great piece of Mysterious, Sensuous, and Intimate communication. Then people start talking and you have that miracle of power communication: word-of-mouth.

Personally, I find "word-of-mouth" a silly expression. Where else do words come from? What's important is whose word-of-mouth and why they're talking. Some guy comes up to you on the sidewalk and raves about his mobile phone. We all do the same thing. Step to one side. Never slow down. We can hear everything, but we want to listen to something that matters–from someone we love and respect. So Lovemarks grow on emotional connections rather than just word-of-mouth. As Malcolm Gladwell put it:

> "What I am looking for is someone who is defined simply by knowing more than I do. If I wanted absolutely the best source on computers, I would find someone who worked in the industry. But I don't. Most of us look for someone who has a marginal advantage over us in information. I tend to opt for trust over expertise, and I ask my brother."

Let's look at some of these Inspirational Consumers at work.

Inspirational break

Inspirational Consumers can also help Lovemarks transform products. "Break" is a square chocolate bar with a loyal following in Greece. It had one problem. The blocks were so thick people struggled to break or bite off a piece.

The retailers soon picked up the message from the consumers and let Break know. Consumers wanted a slimmer bar that they could snap. The Break people heard these complaints and acted. The blocks were made thinner and less expensive.

Lovemarks hear messages of Love from Inspirational Consumers when everyone else hears complaints.

Inspirational busybody

In Spain, one Inspirational Consumer participated in the marketing of corporate giant General Mills. A fanatic lover of Old El Paso Mexican food knew that if he was to see his loved cuisine made more readily available, he was going to have to come to General Mills' aid. The road to success, as he saw it, was paying more attention to the local situation. Why call it "Thick 'n Chunky" sauce if the product was "like our Spanish traditional Pisto sauce, but cooked in a Mexican way?"

The Old El Paso products were perceived as too spicy, too difficult to cook, and reserved by the Spaniards for special occasions. But our Inspirational Consumer was convinced that Mexican food could be consumed daily like Spanish paella.

Putting his thoughts down on paper he sent a list of suggestions to General Mills. He pointed out the similarities between Mexican and Spanish cuisine and even offered to write a cookbook that would convince the Spaniards that Old El Paso was easy to prepare.

The result of this inspirational intervention? General Mills marketing managers wrote a textbook happy ending. They made the suggested changes. New labels, new product names and, yes, you guessed it, a cookbook written by Old El Paso fanatics is to be published.

Inspirational grandmothers

Inspirational Consumers want their Lovemarks to be available, not just for themselves, but for everyone. That is their power. When a grandmother in Turkey found that the red cap milk she used was hard to get at the local store, she took action. This Inspirational Consumer looked after her granddaughter, and red cap milk was the only product she felt was good enough for her precious charge. Unfortunately, she and her husband lived on the outskirts of Istanbul, where red cap milk was hard to get. She talked to her local store, rang the sales representative of Sütas, and kept ringing until red cap milk was available locally.

This was fantastic stuff, but then she went that important step further. Concerned that her local store would stop stocking the milk if sales were low, she began a personal campaign. She decorated the store, recruited a group of volunteers to distribute leaflets, and spread the news.

I believe there are Inspirational Consumers like this all over the world just waiting for the call.

Inspirational rustlers

Some Inspirational Consumers are so in Love with their brand they literally can't keep their hands off them. This was what Becker's beer discovered in Chile when they introduced a powerful new character, a black sheep with the Becker's attitude.

It was an instant classic. Everybody fell in Love with the Becker's sheep. It became an icon. So much so that our people started receiving calls from retailers saying that their point-of-sale black sheep cutouts were being stolen faster than they could replace them!

Okay, I don't want to encourage people to strip stores, but that is the sort of attitude that can be harnessed for good. Inspirational Consumers want to be close to the brands they love. We need to get out there with them and feed off their energy.

Inspirational snaps

Any brand that wants to become a Lovemark gets no higher mark of recognition than the hours of time Inspirational Consumers put into fan clubs. Of the many Lovemarks that have sprouted such loose but passionate associations, none was more surprising to me than the Russian-made LOMO camera. Old-fashioned it may be. Strange design? Certainly. Loved? You better believe it. On the web there are 25 country, 80 personal, and seven community sites for the LOMO, including the iconic society **www.lomography.com**. LOMO fans even persuaded the St. Petersburg factory to restart production of the fabled LC-A. No one stands in the way of a Lovemark.

Inspiration rereleased

Consumers who were Loyal Beyond Reason persuaded Technics to bring back the fabled Technic 1200 decks. It turned out that DJs so loved this giant of the turntable world that they wouldn't play with anything else. Now the Technics brand approaches Lovemark status for the club scene. Check out the T-shirts, bags, and slip mats bearing the unmistakable line drawings of the Technics decks and other equipment.

So too with Kung Fu ice cream in Denmark.

A local radio DJ convinced over 6,000 Inspirational Consumers to contact local company Van den Bergh to reinstate liquorice-flavored Kung Fu ice cream. Four years later, in 2002, Van den Bergh launched a website where consumers could vote for their favorite ice cream. The inevitable result? Kung Fu, with 51,000 votes.

Inspirational countdown

Perhaps even more fanatical than the LOMO lovers is
the man who is probably the ultimate Inspirational
Consumer: Jim Jetters of Douglasville, Georgia. In
1999, Jim's Toyota Starlet was getting ready to
clock one million miles! Love his car? Sure did.
The Starlet still had the original transmission
and engine and, with regular maintenance,
had been all but trouble-free. Jim wanted
everyone to know it too.

His passion for his Toyota earned him a spot on
the "Late Show with David Letterman" and the audience
got to see the zeros click over for themselves.

And remember, Jim also owns a couple of Camrys, one with 240,000 miles on the clock and
the other 100,000. Jim is counting down already.

Stepping up

Inspirational Consumers are always passionate, forever enthusiastic, sometimes fanatical, and
fiercely loyal. Tapping into their emotional connections can reveal the insights Lovemarks live
off. They do tend to see everything in black-and-white, but this is just the Love shining through.

Seeking out Inspirational Consumers and feeding their innovations back into the design,
manufacturing, marketing, distribution, and sales processes is simple common sense.

Business finds it tough to give up the control relationship they have had with consumers.
This means they have been very reluctant to unleash the power of the Inspirational Consumer.
We are now past unleashing. Those Inspirational Consumers have been empowered hugely by
the Internet, and they are going to use their power in ways beyond anything we can imagine.
Get ready.

By getting close to Inspirational Consumers, I believe any business can transform itself and
step up to become a Lovemark.

We have tapped the voices and opinions of Inspirational Consumers through our website www.lovemarks.com. Here's a selection of what touches the passions and loyalties of people around the globe.

REMO

The antithesis of blah, an on-line Aladdin's cave, the essence of must have and always, but always...fun. It's a reminder of a misspent youth, the excitement of providing the perfect gift, and knowing that the recipient will not be able to resist REMOing in return. Love is a REMO stripey thing!

[Manager, Australia]

IKEA

IKEA is the place where fantasy becomes reality and where adults become children. At IKEA's shop you can jump on the chairs, sleep in the beds, improve your Swedish, invent your house, find free pencils, and leave your babies at the playfield...and it all fits in your car!

[Student, Italy]

Air Tahiti Nui

You step onto the plane, tuck a heavenly scented tiare flower behind your ear, have a glass of French Champagne and lie right back to sleep in a soothing blue cabin, only to be woken before descent by a beaming Tahitian hostess gently touching your shoulder and handing you a hot towel. The first time I flew this airline, I didn't want to get off—even when we landed in Papeete.

[Journalist, U.S.A.]

iPod

I don't go anywhere without mine. I find myself staring at it, admiring it, absentmindedly stroking it, reaching for it in my bag when it is out of sight, toying with it as a nervous habit, anxiously awaiting the opportunity to use it, meticulously searching for scratches on it after I return home from a long day. In fact, I have left in place the original plastic sticker over the white dial, in order to preserve my iPod's pristine perfection.

[Account executive, U.S.A.]

Apple

After 14 years I'm still in love. To be honest, I don't know why I feel this way. I've simply never wanted to give the other ones a go. I don't even really know what the differences are....Well, apart from looks! I've been told both do almost the same things—one way or another. But would they feel the same in the dark? Perhaps deep down I know it's the way you learn to handle them, how readily they respond to your needs....Or maybe there's more to it? Richard Briers/George Clooney. PC/Apple Mac. What sort of idiot would divorce their soul mate? Apple Mac—you are my Lovemark.

[Designer, New Zealand]

A-Channel

The impact A-Channel has on each community it serves is phenomenal. It's not just a TV Station–it serves as a public forum, a charitable organization, and a friend to every Manitoban. A-Channel is LOVED because Love is what it offers. They offer great programming too. There are several stations here in Canada that care about their audience, but A-Channel is so sincere–it spreads its Love-vibe throughout the region. People all over Manitoba have "A"s on display on their homes, cars, kids, and selves and they are all homemade! These people are in *Love*.

[Producer, Canada]

The Statue of Liberty

In times uncertain, past and present, humanity invests her with–or does she already possess?–the strength of a living icon, the hope of a living spirit. I've stood within her skin, climbed her winding stair, and surveyed her domain from her crown. The nobility of her face, her steady gaze, and strong, straight stance keep the faith like nothing else on this planet. Words are not equal to the hope and faith the Statue of Liberty perpetuates.

[Creative director, U.S.A.]

Barbie

The famous fad of the 60s is now a serious Lovemark thanks to the undying Love of young girls everywhere. Barbie taps into their dreams and hopes. She takes them by the hand partway into adulthood, but always in the safe guise of play.

[Editor, New Zealand]

Aveda

Like a bevy of kind, attentive, attractive sisters, my Aveda hair products sit waiting to do my hair right each morning. Dressed in their sweet, subdued colors, the team springs into action to smooth me, hold me, shine me up....Patiently they work to discipline my unruly mop 'til it gleams and hangs just right. They wrap me up in their bright scents and send me out to face the world, knowing deep down that I am loved.

[Educator, U.S.A.]

Twinings

Twinings teas have a special place in my life. I'm just not a morning person, but if, as I wake up to that unfriendly light, I focus on the image of my breakfast tray with its fragrant pot of Twinings Russian Caravan tea, I can make that brave move out from under the covers. Just a cup clears my head, gently, not with a crude rush of caffeine, just a sensitive push into reality. Twinings teas help me face the day ahead with courage.

[Mother, Australia]

Where the Wild Things Are

The greatest children's book ever written. Everyone can identify with Max because there's a little bit of him in all of us. At times we want to escape from something or someone, yet we know in our hearts that the grass is greener where we stand. This book is absolutely timeless and thought-provoking. It will endure forever and will be read and re-read by children and their parents until the end of time.

[Entrepreneur, U.S.A.]

BBC

It was only a few years ago that the BBC booked a one-way ticket to the U.S. on the QE2. It soon became a ray of light amongst the thousands of bland television stations we are bombarded with here in the States. Since that time, my own cultural horizons have grown and matured along with its programming. Ever since crossing over to the "English channel," the word comedy has taken on a whole new meaning, "home decorating" has turned into something of a sport, and my garden (or whatever you call the two-by-two patch of grass in front of my house) has blossomed. My Anglophilia has finally been satisfied.

[Legal assistant, U.S.A.]

Coppertone

In the 60s the fragrant, exotic smell of this lotion, the sun, and the ocean, liberated our coastal backwater. Closing your eyes on a lonely beach in a bikini, you could dream and escape to America, where it was all happening!

[Company director, New Zealand]

Mikimoto

I received my Mikimoto pearls as a gift from my boyfriend of three months back in 1986. Immediately I knew he was a keeper. What a romantic, luxurious gift for a man to give a woman. Forever associated in my mind with images of the beautiful Mrs. Jacqueline Kennedy Onassis and the Queens of England. When I'm wearing them they remind me of my husband's Love for me. I cherish them. I married this man—and two children later, we remain very much in Love!

[Wife and mother, U.S.A.]

BMW motorcycles

BMW motorcycles are a world (and a brand) apart. And so much more than a brand. It is a lifestyle, a way of living, a way of defining myself and the world around me. When I am on my R 1150 GS, traveling through the wild and wonderful corners of Africa, this incredible machine becomes my survival kit. And after hundreds of thousands of kilometers, the "kit" becomes "comrade," and the bond becomes emotional. To me, this brand means freedom. Or breaking free. Escaping. But that is almost generic to all bike brands. The uniqueness of the BMW is that it is a motorcycle for the wild. It turns me, an ordinary man, into an explorer, a pioneer, a Lone Ranger. It makes me more than I am.

[Author, South Africa]

Absolut

It is smart, funny, trendy. It always has a different story for us—inviting us to discover "what is the story this time?" It can be anything it wants, transforming any object, situation, or issue. I don't even drink vodka, but I love the Absolut brand.

[Designer, Romania]

Post-it Notes

Placing a Post-it Note on a page thrills me to my very soul. It doesn't matter if the Post-it is perfectly placed or neatly annotated, it doesn't mind being torn or inked up. A page is not complete unless it has at least one Post-it on it, fluttering delicately, but sturdy enough to stay there no matter how many times I go over the book, no matter how many times I shuffle the pages.

[Proofreader, U.S.A.]

Tiffany's

It's just a little aqua-blue box, but you know that inside is something absolutely special. Could you ever open a Tiffany box without a quiver of excitement over what it contains? No other brand says more about how you feel about someone than this.

[Creative director, Australia]

Birkenstock

A great story: 19th century German cobbler Konrad Birkenstock refines the shape of his grandfather's clog molds and adds a flexible arch support. It wins the support of local doctors. Eighty years later, Konrad's son Karl applies the next-generation innovation and takes the clog one step further–into a shoe. *Voilà*–the Birkenstock sandal is born. I love the classic styling, and most of all I love the comfort. Heidi Klum can keep her "designer collection" denim and rhinestones!

[Builder, The Netherlands]

Bike Friday

If we all rode bicycles, all the time, then we would be happier, healthier, our air would be cleaner, we would embrace our neighborhoods, and we wouldn't start wars over oil. And though not all trains, buses, airplanes, and subways support travel by bicycle, a Bike Friday goes anywhere, packed inside a suitcase. The suitcase turns into a bicycle trailer, giving you complete freedom to travel to any location on the planet. Freedom to move under your own power, whizzing happily along! My Bike Friday is my heart's passion; it makes my heart stronger, my legs more shapely, and enlarges my love for humankind.

[Bicycle advocate, U.S.A.]

Moleskine

Physically, the right size and shape to easily, quietly, and calmly carry around. The notebook is hidden in plain sight. Psychologically, not a container but a purse, a treasure box of thoughts and impressions and feelings and data. A message to myself that need not be mediated by the perceptual idiosyncrasies of others. My playground of the mind and heart. The elastic band serves a dual function of physical closure and psychic mind latch. Possibly its greatest design feature.

[Assistant airport manager, U.S.A.]

Fnac

A specialist seller of books, CDs, and videos, Fnac has around 60 shops all over France. Their main competitors are the big retailers like Carrefour that sell you everything cheaply–from a pound of carrots to TV sets. Fnac, on the other hand, has managed to create a special climate in their stores and a pride in buying cultural products from them rather than from the big retailers. Their assistants know about everything. So much so, it becomes a challenge to question them about a field they don't know! And in every shop, you will find a space dedicated to exhibitions or artist interviews or a showcase of some kind. This makes Fnac not just a place where culture is sold–but also a place where culture happens.

[Manager, France]

Google

Google is my best friend! Google is my best friend! Google is my best friend! Google is my best friend! Google is my best friend!

[Copywriter, Turkey]

Toyota

Here in Egypt I see loved Toyota pick-up trucks every day. Paint jobs don't last well in this climate with sand being such a big problem. It upsets locals that own Toyota pick-ups to find that the large Toyota sign at the back of the vehicle wears out. The answer, for many, is to paint the name "Toyota" in bright colors over the original sign. That way you can show your Love for your pick-up truck and the name Toyota at the same time. These brightly painted signs on the back of pick-up trucks are everywhere to be seen in this city of Cairo and all other parts of Egypt.

[Retailer, Egypt]

Shah Rukh Khan

Shah Rukh Khan is a cosmic human being. He uses the big screen to depict some of life's most poignant moments, and thereby touches the hearts of millions across the globe. He urges you to fall in love, break free, set your sights high, and achieve the impossible. He shows us how you can make your life anything you wish–after all, against the odds, he did! He embraces change and challenge, and believes that even the bad experiences can be learned from. He is one of the most inspirational human beings to grace this millennium. He is Shah Rukh Khan.

[Scheduler, South Africa]

Ermenegildo Zegna

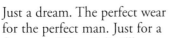

Just a dream. The perfect wear for the perfect man. Just for a few men. When I die I'll want to wear an Ermenegildo Zegna suit so I can be in heaven with all the Ermenegildo Zegna angels.

[Salesman, Costa Rica]

Guinness

It's a hot day, or a cold day, or a mild day...okay, it's *any* day. You stand at the bar and order a pint of Guinness and watch the dance inside the glass unfold as the brew that divides the opinion of drinkers by a chasm gently readies itself to be consumed. A bead of sweat breaks on the brow in anticipation. Then the taste. Pure magic. An Irish love since 1759–and now a world Lovemark.

[Manager, Australia]

Original Tommy's Burger

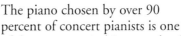

Every time I'm back at Beverly and Rampart, I can't help feeling like I'm 16 again. This was the stop on the way home from Dodgers and Kings games, concerts, shopping, or anything else that would bring me to L.A. for the day. I've seen everything from wedding parties to gang fights, Magic Johnson in his limo to a vagrant on Christmas day who ate a burger I gave him like it was the only thing he'd had to eat in days. Tommy's has had an effect on me like my first kiss, or my first car; it's something that stays with you no matter where you go. For me, Tommy's will always be more than a burger; it's part of my life.

[Graphic designer, U.S.A.]

Steinway

The piano chosen by over 90 percent of concert pianists is one of the great musical Lovemarks. Steinway pianos are lovingly polished, tuned, and cared for through generations. A Steinway brings the past, present, and future together with the mysterious power of music.

[Car salesman, U.S.A.]

BookCrossing

These are dark days, in which most news seems to be bad, and truth is hard to identify. So the fact that there are so many people all over the planet whose love of reading and spirit of generosity and playfulness is alive is not just good news–it's wonderful news. In the long run, encouraging people to read may be the best way to rescue the world from this confusing twilight. When people read enough, they learn. They think. And then, we hope, they act responsibly. BookCrossing has given me hope, for which I am deeply grateful. Telling others about it is a delight–I feel that there is no gift more valuable than involving others in this movement.

[Management consultant, U.S.A.]

Mini

My first car was a Mini. I bought it with money saved from my first job. She had the old sliding windows and side windows with the clips. My dad absolutely hated the transverse engine because he had to take the radiator grill off each time it needed maintaining. I grew up with that car. It saw me through college and brought me home on weekends. She finally went to the big car park in the sky the day I got married. She failed her MOT and was too expensive to repair. It was like losing an old friend–I cried buckets for that car. Even today, seeing a Mini makes me smile and the newly relaunched Mini deserves to capture the heartstrings of a whole new generation. She's fun, sassy, and independent.

[Management consultant, U.K.]

Doc Martens

Docs signified teen angst and rebellion for me and all the other kids growing up in suburbia. When I started wearing them my parents didn't get it. For girls, Docs showed the world that for the first time "cool" meant more to you than "pretty" and you were developing your own sense of style. True, all your friends wore the same shoes, so your style wasn't necessarily original, but it was getting there. At least I didn't dress like my parents!

[Stylist, U.S.A.]

Singapore Airlines

I love the way they let me sleep through the (fantastic) food service and then when I wake up in the middle of the night, they bring me a bowl of great noodles. Complete bliss–and no fuss.

[Consultant, U.K.]

Snaidero

Snaidero was the first to understand that kitchens are evolving from a place where you cook and eventually eat, into a place where you transform food into Love and affection for yourself and your family and friends. Famous designers have worked for them. Their new ES kitchen is made in such a shape that it can be put anywhere–even in front of a window. It feels smooth and functional and it follows the curves of your body when you flex yourself in one of your favorite sports–cooking!

[CEO, Italy]

1. Get out of the office. Your Inspirational Consumers won't come to you – and they don't live in the office down the hall.

2. Ask the great questions. Write down a list of six questions that will stimulate your customers into talking to you Keep the list in your pocket or close at hand wherever you go.

3. Be passionately curious. About _everything_.

4. Be an Inspirational Consumer yourself. Get into an emotional relationship with a brand or product you love See what happens from the other side.

5. Find half a dozen Inspirational Consumers for your own business. Ask them round for a meal and get to know them and what makes them tick.

Five things
to do tomorrow

Chapter 15
ROLLING THUNDER

At Saatchi & Saatchi, we've been putting Lovemark ideas into practice. We want to make as many Lovemarks for our clients as we can. We know that any business that is not creating Lovemarks is simply not creating value. Here are case studies on Olay, Brahma, Lexus, Cheerios, and Tide from our ideas people from around the globe. Each one of these stories dramatically demonstrates the power of harnessing the Lovemark characteristics: Olay using Mystery to launch into a tight market; Brahma wrapping up the beer market with the power of storytelling; Lexus dealers building empathy with customers; Cheerios and Tide repositioning themselves as consumer icons.

OLAY
A Mystery story

What do you do when you are so successful that your loyal band of consumers don't want you to change? When you know you are limited by the category, but the ones who love you most won't let you move?

This was Olay in 1999. A great product, well-loved, and the leader in mass-market sales of mid-priced moisturizers.

But one huge, new area remained for Olay to break into: the prestige skin-care market—the world of supermodels, movie stars, and beauty queens. A sector that

accounted for nearly 40 percent of the global skin-care market. And, critically, a step up to premium prices.

The stakes in this market are high. With them come the desire to stay young. Or, even more profoundly, the quest to fend off mortality.

The prestige sector had been dominated for years by the Big Beauty Industry Players. They played hard. Their advertising–arrogant, self-assured, confident–played on consumers' hopes and dreams. Surely, prestige consumers whispered to themselves, the stuff you pay a lot of money for is more likely to work. And the stuff you pay less for? Got to be a little less effective. Millions of women throughout the world had listened to this "logic" for decades.

The prestige sector also had service on their side. Department stores are where the expensive luxury brands reign. That's where the beauty consultants ("dragon ladies" with vermilion lipstick and perfect skin) lie in wait, ready to grab a woman's hand and persuade her that the product is perfect for her.

Olay, on the other hand, lived in the "self-select" section of the market–pharmacies, drugstores, even supermarkets. There, with no help in sight, a woman had to feel something about the product before she got anywhere near the store.

The power of 1 and 2…
Olay entered this complex situation with a long and valued history with women… and a trump card. A new anti-aging cream with superb performance. Plus, P&G knew they could make this superior level of performance accessible to more women than ever before. They could, in some cases, offer their cream at up to $100 less than comparable products sold in department stores.

At Saatchi & Saatchi, we figured there had to be a way to capture the best of both worlds.

1. To up-sell the traditional "self-select" consumer, and 2. to entice the prestige consumer off her luxury-brand pedestal…

…equals 3: Enter a whole new beauty opportunity, masstige! Prestige products for the mass market.

Respect before Love
The first job was to make sure that this fantastic product was greeted with the Respect it deserved.

To take Olay into the heart of the prestige skin-care market, the credibility of real opinion formers was critical. These are the beauty editors, the mavens, and the media types. Those super-stylish, trendsetting fashionistas from New York and London.

But how to get these high-flyers to listen? Our team knew that if we said, "Here's a moisturizer that is proven to be more effective than all those other brands…and it's from Olay," we'd get a "yeah, right" kind of response–and that would be that.

What was needed was a breakthrough insight that would not only make these professional influencers notice the product, but also fall in Love with it.

We looked to Lovemarks and found just the thing: Mystery.

The aura of the unknown
The first task was to convince the opinion-leading editors to trial the new product, but without the brand name. They agreed. The result was spectacular.

"I call it amazing effects because it does exactly what it says it will do. I am hooked." "Fantastic. Where can I get more?" "To my amazement the area under my eyes isn't as crinkly as it usually is." "I am really starting to glow now. When I put it on my face it feels like a part of my skin that I have been missing. It is nice to be reunited with a youthful glow again. I'm happy!"

Mystery raised interest and expectations. Testers really did fall in Love with the product.

And although they were surprised when they found out who was behind the Mystery, they were not disappointed.

Our intuition was that the same enthusiastic support could be created with consumers as well. A series of trials and tests confirmed the hunch that Mystery was an inherent part of the success of this fledgling product.

Perceptions of the value of the product–with and without the association of the Olay name–were very different.

Without the Olay name, some women told us they would be willing to spend up to $60 for the product. That was three times more than the price Olay intended taking to market!

With the Olay name attached, the acceptable price point came way, way down.

Clearly, while associations with the Olay name were very positive, it was not a brand that could exist alone outside of mid-tier pricing. For this new product to break into the prestige market it needed something more. And so the launch of Total Effects.

To the power of seven
In developing the concept of Total Effects, Mystery was a guiding light. Take the use of myths and icons. The promise to "Fight the 7 Signs of Aging" evoked all the iconic associations of the number seven. As a visual identifier, we created a graphic of the number seven that was used for three years around the globe.

The moment of Intimacy–and truth
Equipped with the expert testimony of the beauty industry influencers, Total Effects was ready to launch and to take on the prestige sector. The campaign started in the heart of the beauty business: *Vogue* magazine.

Real women who'd participated in the initial trials were recruited and photographed. The spreads were beautiful–but, crucially, believable. The Total Effects launch was a phenomenal success, proving the ability of Olay to attract the elusive prestige consumer. Sales were 53 percent higher in sophisticated prestige markets such as New York, Los Angeles, and Chicago.

And the figures kept on growing, long after the initial marketing campaigns were over. Unlike 92 percent of new product introductions, Total Effects' sales grew in the second year, and even more dramatically in the third year.

Olay has always been respected and loved. With the addition of Mystery and Intimacy, it was also able to make a dramatic leap in price point with the launch of Total Effects.

Brazil–where the beer comes from

Everyone in Brazil knows Brahma beer. After all, they have had well over a century to get acquainted. Brahma was founded in 1888, and has built its position to be the leading brewer in the nation. The name says it all: Brahma *is* "beer."

In 1990, most Brazilians would have said Brahma was a Lovemark.

Brahma was the leading brand, with 35 percent market share. A year later, Brahma decided not just to be out front, but to make everyone know about it. They adopted the line "The Number 1." Confident, assertive– and focused on the beer and its leadership of the market. Trouble was, there was nothing in there about the people who drank it.

Seven years later, Brahma had learned the big Lovemarks lesson:

Love cannot be taken for granted.

The line "The Number 1" created confusion. Was it the first beer to be made in Brazil, the best beer, the leading beer? Who knew and, more and more, who cared? Brahma suffered a hefty 11 percent drop in market share.

Facing up to the truth, Brahma understood it had become too traditional for the young people who consumed it–their largest market. For many, it was no longer about having a good time or self-indulgence.

Brahma's return to the embrace of younger consumers is a textbook Lovemarks story.

To get back in touch, Brahma and F/Nazca Saatchi & Saatchi reached for Sensuality and, more specifically, for sound.

In the search for a moment of real emotional connection with the Brahma drinking experience, the sound of a can being opened was perfect.

"Tsss" became the sound of good times, the sound of anticipation, and the sound of Brahma. The power of sound as an iconic element in a campaign had immediate results.

"Tsss" became part of the vernacular of young Brazilian drinkers. Walk into a bar. Make the sound. You get what you wanted without saying a single word. You were instantly part of a club of fans. "Tsss" became an icon in its own right.

Brahma had nailed sound, but did not ignore the other senses. Specially decorated cans were produced for popular Brazilian parties and festivals. Touch was picked up on with thermo-sensitive stickers that changed color as the beer cooled. And Brahma was sold in champagne-sized bottles in a stunning visual surprise.

Individually these senses-based actions were smart, but more important was what they achieved together. Brahma was dramatically repositioned as physical, with excitement in its sound and touch, and as an essential part of the action. Now that was something that every young Brazilian could relate to on an emotional level.

Having created a physical bond through the senses, F/Nazca Saatchi & Saatchi and Brahma looked to utilizing more Lovemark characteristics–great stories, mythic characters, empathy, and passion.

As Benjamin Franklin once famously remarked, "Beer is living proof that God loves us and wants us to be happy."

That was certainly the spirit that sparked Brahma's turtle campaign, one of the most successful marketing ideas to connect with Brazilians.

The turtle spoke to the hearts of Brazilians. The turtle was irreverent, colorful, surprising…and he loved to party. This was a character that reflected every young Brazilian's ideal image of the national personality.

The original commercials featured the turtle's efforts to find a Brahma beer on a hot, dusty road. The turtle was an animated character interacting with real people and real situations. This freed up the campaign to heighten the action on-screen, and to make absurd juxtapositions.

The first turtle spot was a big hit. People couldn't get enough of the thirsty turtle who hijacks a truckload of beer in his quest to get a Brahma and to get up-close and intimate with some beautiful women at the same time.

F/Nazca Saatchi & Saatchi and Brahma under-stood that beer was part of the consumer's emotional landscape. That being the case, they reasoned, the more Lovemark elements that could be drawn on in the commercial, the more potential there would be for an emotional response. Working through the key Lovemark qualities, the turtle and his world are rich in Lovemark touchpoints.

Mystery: The creation of the turtle's personality was inspired. This was how Brazilian youth themselves wanted to be. Irreverent, inclined to show off, decisive, very successful at achieving goals that are daring and tinged with danger.

The stories of the turtle's escapades were classically constructed. The turtle has a problem: he is hot and tired and trapped in an unwelcoming environment. He sees an opportunity and seizes it. He thus reaps the reward of a cold Brahma beer.

In the early twentieth century, the scholar Georges Polti undertook an extensive review of world literature, and concluded that there are only 36 fundamental stories. The turtle's daring narrative of problem-opportunity-action-success must be one of the world's favorites. It taps into the dreams of every human being: the search for good fortune.

The turtle then became a hugely popular character in his own right. An icon for Brazilian attitude and humor. So intense was the passion for the turtle that his creator, Fabio Fernandes, became concerned that the turtle might become bigger than the brand.

Sensuality: The turtle is highly physical. He may have become a symbol of thirst, but his juggling and balancing of the beer cans delighted everyone with its crazy skill and dexterity. As for sound, the turtle's delighted "iiiih" victory cry became part of the Brazilian vernacular.

Intimacy: The turtle's personality responded to what consumers wanted most in a friend. The level could be exaggerated, of course, but humor and irreverence were highly valued by younger consumers. They felt the turtle was one of them.

After three turtle spots, F/Nazca Saatchi & Saatchi felt the series had done its work. The client had other ideas. Enchanted by the success of the turtle and the emotional response it had created with the people of Brazil, Brahma asked for one more turtle spot.

This one would be special. The commercial would support the Brazilian soccer team, which was playing to qualify for the 2002 FIFA World Cup in Korea and Japan. At the time, no one rated them as potential winners of the Cup.

The new spot encouraged everyone in Brazil to support the underdog Brazilian eleven.

As Brazil's chances improved, it was almost inevitable that another turtle spot was called for.

The turtle had to keep going with the team itself. He had gone from being a mascot to a lucky charm.

Against the odds, the Brazilian team won the World Cup–and Brahma was with them all the way. Many Brazilians could not help but give the turtle some small credit for this remarkable victory.

The effect of creating such a strong emotional tie with the consumer had dramatic results for Brahma. The turtle ad, with its humor, personality, and empathy, achieved an incredible 59 percent awareness during the World Cup. This represented an average increase of 7 percent over the full campaign. Brahma's brand consideration also increased by 4 percent; Brahma had achieved the highest recall and preference in all product categories in Brazil. During the World Cup, audience recall peaked at just under 50 percent–a massive increase from the more usual 5 to 15 percent.

A new luxury car for America? You've got to be kidding!

It is hard to believe now, but as recently as the 1980s, the automotive giant, Toyota, was little known in the United States. Back then, the company was known as a manufacturer of well-priced, small cars. And even in the 80s, "made in Japan," the great put-down of the 60s, still lurked in corners of the trade.

In Japan, Toyota ruled, but the company needed expansion outside the Pacific. The American car market was huge. Winning the hearts of Americans was crucial if Toyota was to meet its growth expectations, and Toyota fully intended to do just that.

Did they do it? They certainly did. During the past few years, Toyota's sales and profits have climbed.

They have achieved their goal to become the most profitable automotive company in the world, and are now pursuing an even higher goal: to become the world leader in global automotive sales.

A big part of this success can be tied to the creation of Lexus, a luxury Toyota brand specifically built for Americans. The introduction of Lexus demonstrates the critical importance of local connections and insight in developing powerful global brands. It also highlights how relationships–the beating heart of a Lovemark–can be the foundation for long-term competitive advantage.

How Toyota turned the tide of consumer opinion from mistrust, through Respect, to Love is a classic Lovemarks story.

Leading with the local

In the 70s and 80s, Toyota had risen to the challenge of convincing a nation of Americans, in Love with American cars, to buy and drive Japanese. Sales of small cars were booming, and Toyota had begun to diversify the lineup. But the introduction of Lexus–a luxury car and a luxury distribution channel that would take on the big European and American manufacturers–was, to say the least, a bold move. The initial reaction? Scorn and disbelief.

Toyota knew the Lexus was up to the job of dominating the luxury car market. They also knew they had some powerful allies in the task of convincing Americans to change their traditional views–car dealers. Such was the Respect that Toyota had built up with its own car dealers, as well as that of the automotive industry in general, they were

confident that people would clamor for the chance to acquire a Lexus franchise. And they did.

Mike Sullivan, a die-hard car sales professional from Santa Monica, California, had worked with Volkswagen, Hyundai, and Isuzu. In 1988, he heard about Toyota's plans to establish a separate Lexus channel:

"There were literally thousands of applicants. Without seeing the product or knowing much about it, other than that it was Toyota's upscale division, people were throwing themselves at the Lexus rep for the opportunity to be awarded a franchise.

"We got in the long line and started negotiating. We jumped in and spent, at the time, a lot of money for a very exciting 'maybe.' It was sort of blind faith–in hindsight, a labor of Love."

With so many dealers keen to come onboard, Toyota could afford to be selective.

Understanding the power of relationships, they saw their dealers as business partners whose own success was integral to that of the company itself. Toyota saw them as people with whom they intended to build a mutually beneficial, long-term relationship.

So how did Toyota select their future partners? "This was before all the surveys, and it was sort of gut instinct as to who wanted to move forward and change the industry with them," says Sullivan. "We simply embarked on a 'no rules' service situation. Of course, the Lexus was an unbelievable car. But more importantly, Toyota didn't say no to us. Even if there was a problem, they'd say, 'Well, fix it for the customer, and you and I'll work out the details later.' They didn't tie our hands with having to argue with the customer over what was perceived to be wrong. If the customer was upset, we were supposed to fix it. And we did."

Dan Davidson has been with Toyota since he started washing their cars in 1968. Dan was another one of the lucky few to be welcomed into the Lexus dealer fold. "Toyota kept the number of dealers to a minimum, which allows us to sell quite a few cars per outlet, and for us to be profitable. With that profitability we're able to give the customers that little bit extra. And we're able to keep reinvesting in the service side of our business."

Customers own the brand
Toyota's corporate focus on "QDR"–Quality, Durability, Reliability–is legendary. These elements of Respect are now tablestakes in the automotive industry.

If everyone is respected, everyone is the same. The task then is to step up beyond Respect and form a relationship created out of emotional connections. This sort of bond requires sensational service.

With a commitment to service, Lexus dealers set new standards that other dealers struggle to match. Does it work? You only need to ask Lexus owners. Service has become a hallmark of the Lexus brand.

Mike Sullivan endorses the "little things" that add up to a big difference. "The free car washes, the fresh rolls, the Starbucks coffee, the leather chairs with the Internet service…there's no one tangible thing. It becomes the whole experience."

At Longo Lexus, there are no customers, only guests, states Tom Rudnai. "We treat every guest like a guest in our home. We have relationships that grow with every visit to our facility and we are very respectful of our guests' time. We want to meet and exceed expectations every time a guest comes to Longo."

Dan Davidson, too, makes superior service a focus of his business. "We offer free pick-up and delivery when servicing or purchasing, via flatbed. And all minor services are performed by roving technicians at the customer's home or office, allowing the customer to make the most of every moment in their busy day.

"Say somebody buys a car from us, and they drive it home, and a few days later a scratch appears on the vehicle, or it gets a crack in the windshield, or a flat tire. Then the customer calls us up, and there's one of two things we can do. We can say no, and make the guest feel uncomfortable. Or we can replace the windshield or the tire, and it may cost us a couple of hundred bucks. And we do that. We say, no problem–when would you like it? Do you need a loaner car? We'll take care of that Guest. We have an advocate for life."

Listening Beyond Reason

Lexus dealers offer a conduit to the consumer–but as in all successful relationships, the communication is two-way. Dealers are regularly consulted about improvements. They're often called on to coordinate customer focus groups, which are more like family gatherings, to gather valuable product feedback.

But unlike some other manufacturers, Toyota takes this feedback onboard. This generates a feeling of trust that perpetuates the willingness of dealers and consumers to give back to the company–a virtuous cycle that keeps the relationship alive and growing.

Says Dan Davidson, "Toyota's Lexus people listen, they truly listen. Other companies probably conduct the same sort of meetings. But what do they do with the information? You might as well not have bothered with the meeting, because the manufacturer is just going to go down the path they're already going.

"Lexus is different. Every single car that comes out, we're asked to contribute our knowledge to its development. They want to know the things that are really important to the consumer."

We've learned a great deal from participating in the Lexus start-up. Like Saatchi & Saatchi, Toyota believes that Nothing is Impossible. And like us, they too understand the power of Loyalty Beyond Reason–the very loyalty they created with Lexus owners.

Out of the bowl and into the heart of the family

Breakfast is big business in the U.S. Think $8 billion a year. And that's the ready-to-eat cereal category alone. How much do Americans love their cereal? Beyond reason. And, at the heart of this passionate morning-time Love affair is General Mills' cheery little O in its bright yellow box.

When breakfast cereals first appeared on American tables in the 1940s, Cheerios was there. At that time, cereal was a commodity product based on grain forms. Corn Flakes and Rice Krispies from Kellogg's. Wheaties, Corn Puffs, and Cheerios from General Mills. Back then, these five originators shared a powerful 75 percent of the cereal market.

Today the cereal business is packed with over 250 brands, and market share has declined accordingly. But in spite of this dramatic shift, Cheerios remains a Number One, a Lovemark that has lived through the history of cereal itself. This is a brand that has built such powerful emotional connections with consumers that any American from six to 60 would recognize its distinctive shape and most likely recall having eaten Cheerios cereal at some time in his or her life.

Commodity to brand

How did Cheerios do it? How did the cereal manage to thrive in this fiercely competitive category? To begin with, General Mills realized early on that food purchases are rarely ever about what's in the box, the package, or the can.

The deciding factor is about what the consumer needs in his or her life.

Back when cereal was still a commodity, consumers eating breakfast wanted little information beyond what type of grain they were consuming. Wheat, rice, or oats was about as far as things went. Later, people needed to know just what differentiated one grain from another, and breakfast eaters began to choose from a wider range of criteria: taste, texture, color, size, and shape. Some exceptionally effective advertising bylines were born at the breakfast table. The great "Corn Crunch" and "Snap! Crackle! Pop!"

General Mills was one step ahead. They took their messages further—out of the bowl, and into the lives of their core consumers. Focusing strongly on "higher" values of health and nutrition, Cheerios was established as both relevant and salient for adults. Pediatricians recommended Cheerios as the ideal first solid food for babies. Studies showed that children who ate a healthy breakfast did better in school. And oat bran was shown to reduce cholesterol and promote a healthy heart. Great news for the dominant oat cereal on the market.

O is for Optimism

The rational, health-benefit message worked to establish Cheerios firmly in the minds of consumers as "The One and Only" whole-grain cereal that was best for the family. So far, so good. This powerful, product-based proposition sustained Cheerios through two generations, positioning it as the Number Three brand in the category, with an average 3.3 share.

But in the late 1990s, General Mills, along with the other big cereal manufacturers, became alarmed. 1998/99 had marked the third straight year of sales decline for breakfast cereals—the longest decline in the history of the business.

To make matters worse, new cereal competitors continued to proliferate, dangerously eroding the big players' share. And to shore up losses, many of the key cereal manufacturers moved away from long-term, brand-building initiatives, pouring marketing dollars into tactical sales promotions and price incentives.

Advising General Mills, Saatchi & Saatchi convinced the company that emotion, not information, was the key to long-term success. The way forward was to transform Cheerios from a breakfast cereal into a member of the family. The campaign would focus on the person most closely associated with the emotional moments of breakfast time–Mother. From extensive research, and years of speaking to her with rational messages, Saatchi & Saatchi and General Mills already knew what was going on in her head. The next step was to capture her heart.

Brand to Lovemark

A new campaign was created to build on the Respect Cheerios had gained, adding a crucial new ingredient. Love.

Rational product claims were carefully examined and translated into how a mother might respond to them emotionally. This understanding formed the basis for a series of TV spots and print work showing Cheerios in intimate family situations.

In the series, Cheerios was presented as emotional support to a mother's innate sense of nurturing, as well as pervasive in her children's growing up. Cheerios stood in as both the opportunity to connect within the family, and the child's need to fly. And the adult-focused, healthy-heart message became the brand's recognition that all parents want to be there for their loved ones as they grow up.

Bigger than breakfast

The results of the campaign were dramatic. Sales grew an average of 4.1 percent in volume, representing a year-on-year increase of about $75 million. And share leapt to an average of 4.4 percent, taking Cheerios from Number Three to Number One in breakfast cereals.

By positioning Cheerios as a member of the family, Saatchi & Saatchi and General Mills were able to capture the emotional power behind the brand's powerful heritage. The result was the transformation of common oats to an enduring expression of a mother's Love for her family.

Time and Tide

Generations of Americans grew up with the smell and feel of clothes washed in Tide. The box with the bull's-eye was emotionally connected to the memories of families throughout America. The crispness of a father's shirt. The smell of fresh, Tide-cleaned linen desperately missed in the cold bed of a college dorm. Sheets flapping on the family line. Tide was the scent of a family that cared.

These were the family-oriented values that had carried the Tide brand for decades. Since 1946, when Procter & Gamble introduced the world's first synthetic laundry detergent, Tide has led its category far ahead of its nearest competitor.

But by the late 90s, Mom was more likely to be up to her elbows in paperwork than suds, and nostalgia was no longer powerful enough to grow the brand. In a new era of instant gratification, sales stagnated. Tide was starting to be perceived by consumers as a mass-market product, out-of-touch with the realities of everyday lives.

P&G knew that Tide could still work sensual wonders in the laundry. They also knew that washing clothes remained a ritual act of caretaking, an activity that helps keep families functional and in harmony.

Four issues stood out. How to:
- increase the relevance of the brand
- re-establish the close relationship that Tide had forged with the family
- make Tide a Lovemark for the contemporary generation and beyond
- demonstrate that Tide understood the very diverse needs and values of consumers

The challenge was to get intimate with a whole new group of consumers.

The first thing that P&G and Saatchi & Saatchi did was to take a long, hard look at the lives of what P&G affectionately calls "Moms."

It became apparent that, while family was no less important to them than it had been for their own mothers and grandmothers, the way they cared for their families had changed. And it had changed radically.

Moms on the move
Today's women live their daily lives on a punishing schedule. They deliver their children to and from school. Their days are often packed with events and extracurricular activities. Then there is the planning and participating in family events on the weekends and running the household. Added to this marathon is the fact that the majority of mothers work full- or part-time. They live in their cars. They're constantly on the move.

Clearly, Tide could no longer talk to these women in the way it once did–she didn't stand still long enough! The brand would have to catch her on the run–out in the world, not in the home, where its advertising messages had traditionally reached her.

The message would have to be clear and quick. A message that showed how the brand empathized with her hectic and demanding lifestyle.

Point of Dirt

All mothers are familiar with the placement of point of sale candies, gum, and small toys at the checkout within tantalizing reach of small eyes and hands. The easy purchases you just can't resist in a moment of weakness.

To talk with Tide's consumers, we developed the "Point of Dirt" campaign. This, we figured, would represent all the classic situations where spillage and staining occur. In the car. On the bus. At the pizza parlor. A myriad of places.

The strategy was to have Tide speak to mothers at the Point of Dirt–and to reassure her that in that instant, Tide would be right alongside her to clean up the mess.

The advertisements that Saatchi & Saatchi created were light-hearted. Optimistic. Amusing. Ads that brought smiles to the faces of mothers and everyone else who identified their own personal sticky situations with the stories on the billboards.

As one consumer told us: "Everybody's been there. It's so appropriate."

Another: "I think it's more personal when they speak to you at that moment. It's almost as if they knew what you were doing."

The campaign was a rare and successful fusion of medium and message. An intriguing blend of information and Intimacy. The reward? Sales showed an immediate leap, and continued to grow year-on-year, in some markets up to 25 percent.

Now that's a dramatic turnaround for a brand that was running out of energy. By listening to the consumer, we created a very special moment of Intimacy–a moment that reveals emotional understanding. A moment that proved to be the foundation of returning a brand–Tide–to its status as a true and enduring Lovemark.

Chapter 16

WHAT THE WORLD NEEDS NOW

At the start of this book I described the restlessness that pushed me from job to job and led me to Saatchi & Saatchi. My belief that emotional connections are critical to the future, combined with Saatchi & Saatchi's mantra that Nothing is Impossible, has unleashed a powerful force–Lovemarks.

Our world needs Love. It needs optimism and inspiration if we are to deal with the pressing problems we face. The severe hardship experienced by over two billion human beings. Conflicts, disease, corruption. Sometimes these problems feel overwhelming, but as people in the world of business, we cannot look away. The world of business can lay claim to many fantastic achievements, but we must never forget our involvement in many of the problems. And more importantly, we must commit ourselves to finding solutions.

I believe that the role of business is to make the world a better place for everyone. First, by creating self-esteem through jobs, choices, opportunities, and challenges. And then by focusing our creative minds on innovating for the greater good.

When I grew up in the industrial northwest of England, we had no money and few options. Those were decades of economic and social decline and, as painter Willem de Kooning observed,

"The trouble with being poor is that it takes up all your time."

Anyone who has lived in a poor community knows that the most crippling effect of unemployment is the loss of self-esteem. There is a simple logic at work here. You create self-esteem by creating employment. And so the purpose of business, no matter what any economist tells you, is to create self-esteem.

The past informs, but it cannot be changed. My concern is the future. How can business navigate self-interest towards social interest? How can we mobilize the innovations born of corporate Research and Development for the benefit of many? How can business create a tipping point that sets a course for human well-being?

Any business must make sense economically, but there are now new imperatives. It must also be environmentally and socially sustainable over time. The planet, people, and profits. All for one and one for all. We need to guarantee to our children that the foundations are in place for sustainable enterprises across all dimensions.

Can business do this? I believe it can. It sure has the credentials! As I tell business students around the world, business is the engine of human progress. If you want to change the world, you're in the right place. Why? Because the people who will lead the innovation and create the opportunities that build and transform lives will be the ones who dream about, obsess over, and plan the flow of goods, ideas, and experiences.

And what is it that makes the heart of business beat? People. The desire of people all over the world to choose products, services, and experiences that satisfy their needs, fit their values, engage their emotions, and respond to their desires. To substitute functional over-the-counter transactions for the warmth of genuine emotional connections. When they find such connections, I have seen consumers transform from fickle brand-hoppers to fiercely loyal advocates. As you know from Chapter 14, I call these people Inspirational Consumers—the passionate guardians of a Lovemark.

This is the new reality. A world that not only demands that businesses be up-front and transparent, but also insists that consumers be truly at the center. In such a world, producers who embrace consumers and communities by building Respect and inspiring Love can anticipate premium rewards. Producers who don't will be sidelined and, over time, displaced.

I often ask people whether they'd rather work for a company that is liked, or one that is loved. One hundred percent go for Love. With more of their time spent working, people want that work to mean more to them. They are searching for identity and they are determined to make a contribution.

Great companies respond to this demand by articulating a higher purpose. They inspire their people with a call to action that builds identity, focuses on inclusiveness, excites passion, and challenges possibility. And, no doubt, a rock-solid foundation from which it is possible to make the world a better place.

Even the hard neural sciences are finding evidence through brain scans that cooperating and feeling that we are doing the right thing can really make us *feel* great. In *The New York Times*, Natalie Angier summed up Dr. Gregory S. Berns' findings:

"The small, brave act of cooperating with another person, of choosing trust over cynicism, generosity over selfishness, makes the brain light up with quiet joy."

It seems we are wired to cooperate. And what greater project do we have to cooperate on than making the world better for all of us?

This is the philosophy I can see taking root at Toyota–a huge and successful company determined to make fundamental change, and understanding that such change pivots on the commitment of Toyota people. Working with passion and dedication, they are committed to a more prosperous society in this new century.

Positive steps toward a better future are being taken by businesses everywhere. An example? Research and Development that was once corralled at corporate HQ is increasingly being undertaken where it will be applied, where it can make a difference. But let's go further.

I believe that international companies should aim 50 percent of their R&D budget at those 1.3 billion people who earn less than a dollar a day.

This would be a fantastic objective for businesses with a real commitment to inclusiveness.

Will the shift towards business taking more responsibility for the world's well-being be easy? No. As with all shifts of power, there are tough issues to be assessed and resolved. Professor Sandra Dawson, Director of the Judge Institute of Management at Cambridge University in England, highlighted what lies beneath the surface:

"There is a paradox in the sense that if you empower or regenerate, or you enter into a partnership that fundamentally affects the power balance, then it's like a parent and a child. As a parent you enable an independence, which means that a child won't necessarily look at the world the way you do. So if you want to get away from the colonial notion of development, then that means you have to take really high risks, because you are enabling things to happen which may not then seem to be exactly what you would have wanted. In other words, you can't empower and secure regenerative actions and at the same time exercise control."

The desire to control is tough to relinquish, but that is what we must do if we want to start on the journey towards Lovemarks. And let's face it, once you are inspired by the idea of Lovemarks, it becomes impossible to settle for anything less. Tracking Love returns a premium on every conceivable level. As philosopher Daniel Dennett said: "The secret of happiness is to find something more important than you are, and then dedicate your life to it."

Alan Webber, Founding Editor, *Fast Company*:

"One of the things we've always believed at *Fast Company* is that there is a higher road for business to take. That when you combine the notion that work is personal and that outcomes and performance matter, and you hook those two values up to the same energy source, then you actually get the best of all possible worlds. You get a workforce and a team of people who are totally committed to what they're doing. You get better results in their performance and in their sense of what's possible."

At Saatchi & Saatchi, we are determined to expand our sense of what is possible. We have already made our focus "to create and perpetuate Lovemarks through the power of our ideas." We will use our ideas to connect, transform, and empower the people in the 82 countries we operate in. We will demonstrate that to be sustainable in the new century, enterprises will need to take on an emotional dimension. And we will grow stronger because we know that those who engage with more than their own profit margins will gather momentum fast.

Those who limit their benchmarks to rational and financial outcomes will go nowhere slowly.

We have found this to be true in the area of social commitment. Over the years, Saatchi & Saatchi has taken on pro bono work around the world to help social causes. Our response was emotional. Clients would bring us powerful stories of groups and organizations pitched against the most unimaginable social injustice. Child abuse, road deaths, sexually transmitted diseases, war, racism, drugs, torture, lack of contraception, censorship, environmental damage, and many, many more. Our response was to create some of the most compelling ideas in the world.

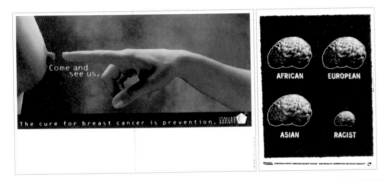

[This girl wants a chat. Lost your patience? Staff nurse Robinson knows it'll soon be a two-way conversation]

Did this make us lose focus on profit? No. Did it dilute our relationships with major clients? Quite the reverse. What it did do was to transform us into one of the world's leading social communication companies. Do our people get a buzz from that and want to do more to set things right with the world? You bet they do.

The more power you give away, the more it comes back to you.

But if business is to make the world a better place we also need to step outside our own comfort zone, share resources, and take a new perspective.

It was this insight, championed by our Worldwide Creative Director, Bob Isherwood, that inspired the Saatchi & Saatchi Innovation in Communication Awards. Literally, a celebration of world-changing ideas.

We are an ideas company, but we know that ideas by themselves change nothing. It's when they go to work and transform the way people live that they matter. Dr. Arno Penzias, former Vice President and Chief Scientist at Bell Laboratories and joint winner of the 1978 Nobel Prize in Physics, lives by this distinction.

"Invention is the product of a creative or curious mind. Innovation is something that changes the life of the customer. It changes the life of the customer in some way, or the world in which the customer experiences things. That's an innovation."

There is a paradox in all this, of course. Often the simplest innovations have the potential to change the world most. This was certainly true of David Irvine-Halliday's invention, which won the Third Saatchi & Saatchi Innovation in Communication Award in 2003.

Dave's idea was born during a trekking trip into the mountains of Nepal. A photonics engineer from Calgary, Canada, Dave was struck by the fact that the villagers in this remote, rural land faced an overwhelming barrier to their health, well-being, and development–darkness.

They had no access to electric light– a situation that confronts some 1.7 billion of the world's people.

Bob Isherwood takes up the story:

"Dave Irvine-Halliday's invention was exactly the kind we had been hoping for when we created the Innovation in Communication Award. What we were after was the application of a simple, practical idea for the greater good. Dave's invention is certainly a simple idea, but the implications for humanity are immense.

"It is based on the amazing power of white light emitting diodes. These tiny bulbs require very little energy but they light up a remarkable area for their size. By clustering a group of these tiny light sources together, Dave took the technology into another realm. He produced a unit that could supply enough light for a child to read by. What a life-transforming idea.

"To me, ideas are the currency of the future. That is the essence of how businesses can make a difference. I agree with Arno Penzias:

"**'Creative people let their minds wander, and they mix ideas freely. Innovation often comes from unexpected juxtapositions, from connecting subjects that aren't necessarily related. Another way to generate ideas is to treat a problem as though it were generic. If you're experiencing a particular problem, odds are that other people are experiencing it too. Generate a solution, and you may have an innovation.'**

"Ideas people start their day, in the words of our technical consultant David Levy, 'looking for trouble.'

"And there is a lot of trouble to find. Large numbers of the people of the world find themselves hard-up against barriers that prevent them from doing simple things that most of the first world takes for granted. I'm thinking of basic activities like being able to read, getting quick, competent medical services, or having access to electricity.

"Our idea? If the lives of millions were burdened by so much trouble, and at the same time ideas people are out there looking for trouble, why not put the two together? That's why we issued the challenge for people to put forward ideas that have the potential to change the way we communicate.

"We weren't thinking of any one kind of communication. It could be anything–from between individuals to between nations and planets! It was, as we say in the ideas business, a very open brief.

"My friend and Innovation Award judge, Edward de Bono, sums it up best: 'It is better to have enough ideas for some of them to be wrong, than to be always right by having no ideas at all....'

"The Innovation in Communication Award is another step towards making the world a better place. It's an example of how curiosity, passion, and concern for the well-being of our planet and its people can inspire miracles."

[Bob Isherwood, Worldwide Creative Director, Saatchi & Saatchi]

A selection of standout entries from past Saatchi & Saatchi Innovation in Communication Awards

Kaspa–Dr. Leslie Kay, New Zealand (Winner, 1998)
A sensory substitute for the visually impaired. The helmet-like device uses sonar signals to help blind people "see with sound."

Self-Adjustable Spectacles–Professor Joshua Silver, U.K. (Edward de Bono Medal, 1998)
An inexpensive eyeglass-lens system destined for the developing world.

Quicktionary–Wizcom Technologies Ltd., Israel (Finalist, 1998)
A handheld "pen" designed to scan text and translate it simultaneously.

Univers Revolved–Ji Lee, U.S.A (Finalist,1998)
A three-dimensional typeface that encourages people to read "in the round."

Peratech–Peratech Company, U.K. (Winner, 2000)
A revolutionary class of electrically conductive composites (QTCs) incorporated into a textile. The fabric, with the unique ability to respond to human touch, has been tested by NASA for spacesuits, and has been used by Burton in "intelligent" snowboarding jackets.

NeuroGraph–Dr. Richard Granger, U.S.A. (Finalist, 2003)
Non-invasive aid for the early diagnosis of Alzheimer's and other neurological diseases.

Mind Switch–Professor Ashley Craig, Australia (Finalist, 2003)
A radical device that turns brain waves into a physical extension of the body, allowing the disabled to operate electronic equipment by remote control.

Artificial Sight–Dr. William Dobelle, U.S.A. (Finalist, 2003)
A pioneering technology using video projection and skull implants, which has resulted in people who have lost their sight being able to "see" after years of total blindness.

The Kinkajou Projector–Design that Matters Team, MIT, U.S.A. (Finalist, 2003)
A mobile library, classroom projector, and teacher-training tool in one–to give remote communities unprecedented access to education.

Stand Up and Walk–Professor Pierre Rabischong, France (Finalist, 2003)
A system of biomedical implants that offers paraplegics the real possibility of walking again.

More about these projects, and about the Award, at **www.saatchi-saatchi.com/innovation**

Judges

1998
Buzz Aldrin–Astronaut and moonwalker
Laurie Anderson–Artist and musician
James Burke–Science writer
Edward de Bono–Inventor of lateral thinking
William Gibson–Science fiction writer
Tibor Kalman–Influential designer
Lachlan Murdoch–News publisher
Richard Saul Wurman–Information architect

2000
Paul Davies–Mathematical physicist and philosopher
Edward de Bono–Inventor of lateral thinking
Brian Eno–Multimedia artist
Kevin Kelly–Founding editor, *Wired*
Pattie Maes–Associate professor, MIT Media Lab
Kjell Nordström–Co-author, *Funky Business*

2003
David Byrne–Musician and artist
Edward de Bono–Inventor of lateral thinking
Danny Hillis–Parallel computing pioneer
Dr. Kenji Kitatani–Vice president, Sony Corporation
John Maeda–Artist and cyberguru
Dr. Story Musgrave–Astro-scientist
Julie Taymor–Film and theater director

To set out to make the world a better place is inspirational.

No inspiration, no innovation. Inspiration is contagious. It is accessible to all. And, I believe, will accelerate us towards a better world.

Sandra Dawson again:

"You can't do it all on inspiration, but without different ideas you can't be good at business. So I think inspiration is absolutely essential. The more diverse your experience, the more you allow yourself to think unusual things, the more different experiences you have, the more you question and the more you look at things from different angles. That's when the ideas begin to flow and where inspiration can be very significant."

To set out to make the world a better place is inspirational. That inspiration feeds back to create more great ideas and actions. This very powerful cycle will not only benefit the people of the world, but everyone who participates. Businesses, individuals, communities, organizations.

Inspiration creates action. It is not about hierarchy, strategy, structure, or systems. It is about people reaching their potential. It is about every individual in an organization exceeding their personal best in pursuit of a unifying dream. People who have the courage to be inspired and to inspire others with such a dream are Inspirational Players. Together, Inspirational Players everywhere stand for Nothing is Impossible.

"The journey of a thousand miles begins with a single step," goes a Chinese proverb. To me, it's not the distance to a better world that matters. The journey is only as long as we believe it to be. What counts are the single steps. The steps taken by Inspirational Players in their path towards creating Lovemarks.

The actions of enterprising people inspired to make a difference through   .

Can business make the world a better place?
Of course it can.

Will business take up the challenge?
It is in our best interests to do so, and let's face it,
our best interests have been a powerful driver for
many centuries.

What can inspire us with the emotional urgency
required to undertake this epic task?

The creation and rewards of Lovemarks.

KR ☺

Index

Other titles by Kevin Roberts

THE LOVEMARKS EFFECT:
Winning in the Consumer Revolution

Kevin Roberts
Published 2006 by powerHouse Books
ISBN: 978-1-57687-267-3

In this follow-up book to *Lovemarks: the future beyond brands*, the voices of consumers, owners, and marketers show the impact of Lovemarks on their lives, their businesses, and their aspirations. *The Lovemarks Effect* offers instruction and inspiration about creating emotional connections, and winning in a consumer-empowered "attraction economy".

Contributors include marketing maverick Tom Peters, Nobel Laureate Arno Penzias, and award-winning writer Malcolm Gladwell. From the business world, interviews with Procter & Gamble's GMO Jim Stengel and Wal-Mart's CMO John Fleming. CEOs from world-winning brands such as Victorinox®, Diesel, and Ben & Jerry's share unique stories about the potential of Lovemarks, and canvass themes from attraction to the in-store experience, and from design to sustainability.

The Lovemarks Effect also showcases the findings of QiQ International's Lovemarks research in a 12-page feature. The study validates the cornerstone qualities that help to propel a brand to Lovemark status, and finds there is conclusive evidence that creating a Lovemark will increase sales, preference, and usage.

From the aisles of the in-store experience to the power of sustainable enterprise, from Lovemarks research to consumer stories, *The Lovemarks Effect* is a joyride through the evolving business landscape.

Titles are available for purchase online and through major retailers.

Trade enquiries should be directed to:
powerHouse Books, 37 Main Street, Brooklyn, NY 11201
Telephone 212.604.9074 Facsimile 212.366.5247
www.powerHouseBooks.com

SISOMO:
the future on screen

Kevin Roberts
Published 2005 by powerHouse Books
ISBN: 978-1-57687-268-0

A new word has been introduced into the global language bank—and this stylish book is its debut. A richly nuanced collection of text and imagery, *sisomo: the future on screen* is a book to conquer hearts and set minds spinning with questions. For business, reaching consumers has become a challenge on the scale of climbing Mount Everest. The mass market is splitting like an Arctic ice shelf, media is fragmenting—and brands have taken a big hit.

This environment presents an unavoidable conundrum for marketers and advertisers as they struggle to find new ways to work. Television, once the shining knight of emotional messaging, is being challenged to explore alternative ways of retaining audiences. A radical shift is also occurring in the relationship between consumers and the media. Where consumers were once passive in the face of the mass market, they are now savvy individuals wired into the greatest information networks the world has ever known.

Enter sisomo—sight, sound, and motion, the combination that made television the most powerful selling tool ever invented. Kevin Roberts says, "There are three keys to the Consumer's heart—Mystery, Sensuality, and Intimacy. Well, here are three more". Saatchi & Saatchi have put sisomo to work on television for decades. Now they are unleashing it in the new world of the Screen Age: on computers, mobile phones, PDAs, in-store displays, and sports stadiums; on screens on the sides of buildings, screens that glow in the corner of our eye.

"Content that engages with sight, sound, and motion is the only way to cut through media fragmentation and connect with today's savvy consumers."
—Kevin Roberts

www.sisomo.com

Further Reading

Diane Ackerman, 1991,
A Natural History of the Senses, New York: Vintage Books.

Diane Ackerman, 1995,
A Natural History of Love, New York: Vintage Books.

John Armstrong, 2002,
Conditions of Love: The Philosophy of Intimacy, London: Penguin.

Donald Calne, 2000,
Within Reason: Rationality and Human Behavior, New York:
Vintage Books.

Antonio R. Damasio, 1994,
Descartes' Error: Emotion, Reason, and the Human Brain,
New York: Avon Books.

Antonio R. Damasio, 2003,
Looking for Spinoza: Joy, Sorrow, and the Feeling Brain, Orlando:
Harcourt, Inc.

Giep Franzen and Margot Bouwman, 2001,
The Mental World of Brands: Mind, Memory and Brand Success,
Oxfordshire: World Advertising Research Center.

Malcolm Gladwell, 2000,
The Tipping Point: How Little Things Can Make a Big Difference,
New York: Little, Brown and Company.

Thomas Hine, 2002,
I Want That!: How We All Became Shoppers, New York:
HarperCollins.

Lynn Jamieson, 1998,
Intimacy: Personal Relationships with Modern Societies, Oxford:
Polity Press.

Regis McKenna, 2002,
*Total Access: Giving Customers What They Want in an Anytime,
Anywhere World*, Boston: Harvard Business School Press.

Margaret Mark and Carol S. Pearson, 2001,
*The Hero and the Outlaw: Building Extraordinary Brands Through
the Power of Archetypes*, New York: McGraw-Hill.

Geoff Mulgan, 1998,
Connexity: How to Live in a Connected World, Boston: Harvard
Business School Press.

David G. Myers, 2002,
Intuition: Its Powers and Perils, New Haven: Yale University Press.

Hamish Pringle and Marjorie Thompson, 1999,
Brand Spirit: How Cause Related Marketing Builds Brands,
Sydney: John Wiley & Sons.

Robert D. Putnam, 2000,
Bowling Alone: The Collapse and Revival of American Community,
New York: Simon & Schuster.

Annette Simmons, 2001,
*The Story Factor: Inspiration, Influence, and Persuasion Through
the Art of Storytelling*, Boston: Perseus Publishing.

Gerald Zaltman, 2003,
*How Customers Think: Essential Insights into the Mind of the
Market*, Boston: Harvard Business School Publishing.

Theodore Zeldin, 1998,
An Intimate History of Humanity, New York: Vintage Books.

Shoshana Zuboff and James Maxmin, 2002,
*The Support Economy: Why Corporations Are Failing Individuals
and the Next Episode of Capitalism*, New York: Viking.

and **www.lovemarks.com**

Credits

Page 13: Photograph © 1966 David Bailey.

Page 40: Lyrics from Cat Stevens' song "Father and Son" are reproduced after consultation with Sony/ATV Music Publishing.

Page 65: Photograph © 1994 Bill Lishman. Bill Lishman is associated with Operation Migration.

Page 92: The GUINNESS word and HARP device are trademarks of Guinness & Co.

Page 96: NIKE and the Swoosh Design Logo are trademarks of Nike, Inc. and its affiliates.

Page 97: Hello Kitty is a registered trademark of Sanrio Co, Ltd, Tokyo, Japan.

Page 98: M&M's is a trademark of Mars Incorporated and its affiliates.

Page 103: This image is an artwork by Christo and Jeanne-Claude: Valley Curtain, Rifle, Colorado, 1970-72. Copyright Christo 1972. Photograph by Wolfgang Volz. The cables in this work span 1,368 feet (417 meters), varying from 365 feet (111 meters) on the sides to 182 feet (55.5 meters) in the center. The artists do not accept sponsorship and pay all expenses of their large-scale, temporary works of art themselves. For more information, visit www.christojeanneclaude.net

Page 116: Photograph of Rowena Roberts by Duncan Cole.

Page 137: Photograph by Kevin Necessary.

Page 155: Photograph by Sung Park, *The Austin America-Statesman*, used with permission.

Page 156: Barbara Kruger, "Untitled" (I shop therefore I am) photographic silkscreen/vinyl, 1987. Courtesy Mary Boone Gallery, New York.

Page 158-59: Photographs with permission from Peter Menzel's *Material World: A Global Family Portrait* (Sierra Club Books, 1994), including image of Wu family by Ka Tai Leong.

Page 167: For further information on King Ken character see www.kidrobot.com

Page 185: Photographs taken for *One In A Billion: An Introduction to the People of China*, written by Sandy Thompson of Saatchi & Saatchi (in production).

Page 209: Photograph by Sarah Maingot.

Page 218-219: CHEERIOS is a registered trademark of General Mills, used with permission. The Cheerios box and still image from the "Football" Cheerios TV spot are reprinted with the permission of General Mills.

Pages 4, 5, 17, 19, 23, 33, 34, 37, 42, 56, 73, 81, 94, 95, 108, 111, 127, 128, 130, 131, 135, 155, 160, 161, 175, 176, 179, 180, 182, 184, 188, 191, 195, 207, 223, and 235 feature images supplied by Getty Images.

Pages 25, 26, 49, 91, 97, 99, 117, 141, 145, 153, 154, 162, and 164 feature images supplied by Corbis.

All terms mentioned in this book that are known to be trademarks or service marks have been appropriately capitalized. Use of a term in this book should not be regarded as affecting the validity of any trademark or service mark.

Any inadvertent omissions to these credits and acknowledgements can be rectified in future editions.

Acknowledgements

This book draws together a range of contributors to inform and shape the evolving story of a future beyond brands.

In beginning to place acknowledgements, my first and biggest credit is to my family. We share a continuous journey from our home in New Zealand to various parts of the world, sustained by human Love. Thank you Ro, Nikki, Ben, Bex, and Dan.

The 7,000+ talented Saatchi & Saatchi people around the world are also family. They have worked together with me to bring Lovemarks to life, and I tell this story on behalf of, and for them.

Credit for the development of concepts for, and execution of, the book's design goes to Derek Lockwood, Saatchi & Saatchi's Worldwide Director of Design. Derek has offered his empathy and energy to give a visual pulse to every page.

Thanks to my friends at SVL in New Zealand, who have been with me every step of the way. Brian, Jane, Jim, Mary, Carla, Simone, Richard, and team....*Chapeau, chapeau*!

The crew at powerHouse Books are entrepreneurial, passionate, and edgy. I've seen how they're a Lovemark to their audiences. And the coolest thing is that they're one block from my office. The pulling power of the local shines yet again.

For the insights given me by those I have spoken with about Lovemarks, and for the generous support I have received from the people I have met and continue to meet, I am grateful.

Many friends helped me during the journey. Inspired me. Opened me. Touched me. You know who you are. Thank you.

Kevin ☺

Kevin Roberts

the future beyond brands

lovemarks

Published in the United States by powerHouse Books,
a division of powerHouse Cultural Entertainment, Inc.
37 Main Street, Brooklyn, NY 11201-1021
telephone 212 604 9074, fax 212 366 5247
e-mail: lovemarks@powerHouseBooks.com
website: www.powerHouseBooks.com

Second edition, 2005

Library of Congress Cataloging-in-Publication Data:

Roberts, Kevin, 1949-
    Lovemarks : the future beyond brands / by Kevin Roberts ; foreword by A.G. Lafley.-- 1st ed.
        p. cm.
    "New expanded edition with new chapter on shopping: diamonds in the mine"--t.p.
    Includes index.
    ISBN 978-1-57687-270-3 (hardcover)
    ISBN 1-57687-270-X (hardcover)
    1. Brand name products--Marketing. 2. Brand name products--Forecasting.
3. Advertising--Brand name products. 4. Trademarks. I. Title.

HD69.B7R63 2005
658.8'27--dc22

                                                    2005014352

Hardcover ISBN 978-1-57687-270-3

Art Direction: Derek Lockwood
Cover Design: Hiroaki Ito
Title Design: Anna Brown
Design Associates: Kiki Bauer, Jen Holley, Holly Tica

Printing and binding by Midas Printing, China

A complete catalog of powerHouse Books and Limited Editions is available upon request; please call, write, or find Mystery, Sensuality, and Intimacy on our website.

10 9 8 7 6

Printed and bound in China

Princess Diana NIDO powdered milk Teletubbies Gandhi Barcelona Dolfin Givenchy Hanes KISS AriZona Green Tea SPEIGHT'S Louis Vuit

PlayStation2 Gisborne Valentino Amnesty International Wizard of Id AMD processors UGG boots Dickies Segway Reef footwear Canada

Altberg Jaguar Ghirardelli Glenmorangie Dodge Line 6 philosophy Nintendo Estée Lauder Annie Lennox J. Lindeberg Teva Kawasaki REA

Television Without Pity Santa Claus Nikon L'O ka TERRE Mykonos Rheingold The Lord of the Rings McVitie's Mandarina Duck 7 UP La A

Whole Foods Kukuxumusu FC Barcelona The New York Times De Cecco pasta Hellmann's real mayonnaise Cheerios Santa Cruz boards Casio

National Public Radio New Balance TiVo Google The Simpsons Doc Martens Necco BBC Aveda NAF NAF London Transport Club Monaco

Arnott's Biscuits BMW motorcycles Campobello Alessi Motorola Calvin Klein Camper Lambretta South Africa Tiffany's Sid Dickens Mem

Sesame Street afri cola Twinings tea Beck's 42 Below vodka AEK Football Club WAKA Kickball Corum Victoria's Secret Boost juice Helmu

Hugo Boss Issey Miyake Hokitika Innocent drinks Entertainment Weekly Siemens ICQ Colo-Colo FC Bagelman's Citibank Murray's Superior

Dyson Gateway computers India Ericsson Lockwood homes Citizen Aqualand Michael Flagg David Beckham Leatherman Radio Dimension

Napster Concorde Symantec PC World Liverpool FC Handspring Treo Wolf Kettler Boy Scouts of America Nirvana Samsung DirecTV Cha

Greyhound Canadian Broadcasting Corporation El Hostal Diamondlot Keith Haring Shu Uemura Telefonica Hermès Winnipeg Blue Bomb

Ryuichi Sakamoto Guideposts magazine EnCirca CJSW Anne Klein II perfume Kiwi bacon Barkers Victoria magazine OnWar Fujiya hotel Th

Corum Bubble watch Tsingtao Moleskine Air New Zealand Iyengar Yoga Mother Teresa Mickey Mouse Light Up The World Foundation T

American Express Coppertone Italy Martin Margiela Parkett art magazine Eames chairs MacPac Bundaberg Ginger Beer The New Yorker N

Prius Amul Asahi Super Dry Burton Versace Banana Republic Absolut The Milky Way Tiffany's Nokia Madonna Yorkshire pudding Lay's

Vigelandsparken The Pillsbury Doughboy Yankees iTunes PEZ Terry Pratchett Bacardi Breezer Simon and Garfunkel Origins Global knive

Mircea Cartarescu Singapore Airlines Golden Gate Bridge Abercrombie & Fitch Budweiser Redwing Castle lager Paulo Coelho Dos Pinos T

Opera web browser H&M One World journeys Canon cameras Marks & Spencer Robbie Naish Lush New York City Captain Morgan's spiced ru

Johnnie Walker Technics 1200 Eukanuba Gary Fisher bikes Flag of St. George illy Biere Larue Pelé La-Z-Boy Salsa Lizano Carhartt Imperial B

Benetton Salt & Lineker crisps Collette Kyoto Huka Lodge Warp records Bavaria Folgers Visa Nutella Sony Gucci All Blacks rugby team

Acqua di Parma Mars Bars President Avenue Fruitworld Porsche Rick Stein LEGO Mini Taj Mahal Ferrari University of Kentucky basketball

Steven Spielberg Hot Buttered Anne Geddes Lee jeans Nescafé The Boss Greece Victory Over Want St. Tropez M•A•C Fnac Sri Ravi Shanka

NASA Triple J Zimtstern Lance Armstrong Kiehls Tumi Dilmah Colin Bell AJAX soccer club Monty Roberts Nike U2 XXXX beer Kenneth Col

Apple The Economist Krispy Kreme Snoopy Swiss Army Barbie Harley-Davidson Gillette Seresin olive oil Audi Bendon Britten motorcyc

Oprah Baileys L&P Bovril Hollywood Tiscali Heinz JC Bamfords Red Bull Trader Joe's Steinlager Old Spice New Zealand Edge Squaresoft

Trung Nguyen iMac Riva boats Guaraná Antarctica Winnie the Pooh Zippo Silver Fern La Quinta Aga ovens Tabasco Chanel No. 5 Snaide

Yahoo! The Olympics Paris Andy Warhol Adobe systems Weleda Coca-Cola Muji Jean Paul Gaultier Upper Deck hockey cards Oreo cookie

Jaws Lockergnome Swiss Miss San Pellegrino Ferrero chocolates Beyoncé Skol Yoo-hoo Slow Food Movement Wrigley's Salon.com Elvis P

Fuel coffee Brooklyn gum Bridgeman Art Library Grateful Dead Mivar portable television Zanussi Umbro San Benedetto Frizzante Tenzan